YOU ARE THE RIVER

Literature inspired by the North Carolina Museum of Art

Edited by Helena Feder

ACKNOWLEDGMENTS

Helena Feder

I AM VERY GRATEFUL to the Mellon Foundation and the American Council of Learned Societies for their generous support. I also wish to thank Katherine White, deputy director of the NCMA, for her kind support of my Mellon/ACLS residency and the many others at the Museum who also assisted with this volume, including Director Valerie Hillings, Senior Editor Karen Kelly, Director of Graphic Design Dave Rainey, Associate Registrar for Collections Michael Klauke, and the Museum's wonderful curators: John Coffey, Linda Dougherty, Jennifer Dasal, Michele Frederick, Caroline Rocheleau, Lyle Humphrey, Maya Brooks, and Amanda M. Maples. Last but never least, I am indebted to my son, Hugh Feder-Clarke, for the hundreds of hours he has cheerfully spent with me in the Museum over the last decade. I look forward to hundreds more.

ARS POETICA

Helena Feder

WRITING AT MY DESK, I often look up at the woman who isn't looking at me.

Jo was sketched in profile with charcoal on paper at a party, perhaps on New Year's Eve, in 1942 (right).[1] Her expression is both pensive and ambiguous. But her style—her high penciled brow and crosshatched upturned wave, the posture of her shaded mandarin collar—suggests the background:

> Everywhere the shining despair of
> ecstasy of the late night's beauty of
>
> bright Bay lights through the fog and
> smoke over martinis and sidecars
>
> sliding color off women's lips open in
> laughter and something a pitch higher
>
> louder as the song goes *anything goes*
> though the whole human world's at war
>
> and still the old joke of lampshades as hats
> because they're all so "lit"—
>
> and Jo in silent profile a portrait
> of no artist's mother no
>
> framed painting no white
> flowered curtain.

The tension in her lips suggests Jo may be the only one in the room not smiling, and I can imagine many reasons. While everyone else raises a glass to Cole Porter's lyric of nudist parties in studios, she's thinking about her closing argument in next week's trial or about the lover who's just sailed into the secret Pacific. Or perhaps she's thinking about her new paintings, passed over for a show in yet another San Francisco gallery. That last story resonates—after all, Jo's at a party with artists. Sometimes I imagine I'm there with her, and sometimes I

John Hoppenthaler

Night Wing over Metropolitan Area

Wing of a blackbird, wing
of a crow. If I seem a vulture,
sometimes, on the wing, adrift

toward carrion, indistinct architecture
of loss, its ambience ... The hydraulic
whine and thud of the landing gear, absence

of towers, moderate tremor of shear
and turbulence. No, not buildings, only
insistent light that props them up; their

corporeal bodies dissolved—enormous
emptiness, which itself is full of color, ghosts
of light beyond emptiness, that which defines them,

that which looms outside the frame, space
between us, the pregnant darkness of our
city, and a million tiny votives that oppose.

The night wing hangs, sags toward you with
gravity, weight of a thousand corpses, screech
of a virus, that shrill hawk as I circle

in a holding pattern, and all I can see is
primary color, pointillism of what's left
behind or flown toward, fugitive colors,

especially the blue rims of your eyes. I lift
or descend, and it seems the same: proximity
may as well be absence; arrival means another

place has been left behind, and I'm taking
off or landing to deliver what support I can.
We are two dark birds, together, keeping

raptors at bay—there, out over the river.

Skunder Boghossian
Night Flight of Dread and Delight

1964
Oil on canvas with collage
56⅝ × 62⅝ in.
Purchased with funds from the North Carolina State Art Society (Robert F. Phifer Bequest)

Bob Siegel

Steerage (a monologue for Jake)

You stood side by side, staring at an endless ocean. Was the old country rotten or the new world a magnet? A lot of time to think and a lot of time to talk, a renowned raconteur, I'm told. Did you share confidences in Yiddish or German?

(beat)

First there was New Orleans and Tillie. Even then, before the bottle, you didn't want him. She made money, you dreamed of revolution, and my father? He was raised in the bayou by Ella. All the kids he played with were black and so he thought he was, too.

(beat)

Trouble with the cops or reveries of greater reckonings, New York called and the little boy came like baggage in steerage. You and Tillie on the Lower East Side, the Jewish tenements. You had money for a tailor shop. Funny, the guy who towered over all the others, the guy who was always on the front line, the guy who always carried the banner on May Day, he was a shop keeper. But the revolution was too slow so a fifth of whiskey upped the tempo. You came home each day and slashed swollen rivers with your strap. I picture my father watching the clock and wondering what he did wrong. I picture Tillie in the next room listening but never thwarting. And you, Jake, the guy who would save mankind, in a frenzied fury, terrorizing a little boy.

(beat)

Another woman, another city, you left. Tillie was no mother, and my dad was left on the street, unclaimed baggage from steerage. He fled the city with no shoes. Let me repeat that, Jake. A twelve-year-old boy crossed the GW bridge barefoot.

(beat)

He worked farms upstate, came back to the city, and became a union man in the garment shops. He read with an appetite that was never full, an uncanny ear for languages, and a knack for telling stories.

(beat)

Years later, married, children, he found you, Jake. Ashamed, he had told mom that you and Tillie were dead. But my brother's Bar Mitzvah brought you out of steerage into the open. He pleaded with you to come. Cropped, shocking white hair, chiseled Teutonic face, and vigilant blue eyes, your hands shook, palsied from years on the steam press or was it the booze. Why did he bring me along? I never asked my father, afraid it would hurt too much. Perhaps a six-year-old would make Jake remember, would open his heart. It didn't work.

(beat)

Years later, my father visited me. We stood at Cooper Union. Now the Lower East Side was the hip East Village. But my dad knew the landmark. A compass, he walked from it as if a needle pointing true north, and I followed, and we found Jake's old tailor shop still standing. Looking through the grimy glass, did he want revenge, sending you back through steerage to some remote burgh? I'll tell you his revenge, Jake. He prospered. He raised a family. He was a gentle man. He never laid a hand on us. We're all doing just fine.

John George Brown
A Tough Story

1886
Oil on canvas
25 × 30⅛ in.
Purchased with funds from the State of North Carolina

Malena Mörling

Not a Ladder, a Door

For her death,
he gave her a door
  to leave through.

Above it,
    the late light
of the sun
    poured down
through the transom,
  finally setting
its gold
    into the earth.

And next to it,
    in a dim corner
of their kitchen,
  he had hung
with string
    whatever meat
was left
    from a deer,
tightly wrapped
  in paper,
grey as ash.

    Because, he couldn't
conceive
    of her not cooking
anything
  over a bonfire
in oblivion.

    Because he didn't
know how to
    prepare for such
an outing.

  Nor could he say
what had been
boarded up
    and splotched,
filled with flecks
    of flying ghosts
in the vicinity
  of a sad
and single morning
    glory.

Gerhard Richter
Station (577-2)

1985
Oil on canvas
98⅞ × 98⅞ in.
Purchased with funds from the North Carolina State Art Society (Robert F. Phifer Bequest), the North Carolina Museum of Art Guild, and various donors, by exchange

Luke Whisnant

Thirteen Ways of Looking at *A Man Scraping Chocolate*

1
Who painted this, no one knows.
And those who once knew
are now dust.

2
Out of ten thousand paintings,
drawings, sculptures, artifacts,
tapestries, photographs, *objets d'art*,
the man scraping chocolate
cries out for inclusion.

From quarantine I download
the digitized image of a painting
I have never seen.
The thing and not the thing.

3
Three dive-bombing blackbirds
sign their names in white splatters
against the museum façade.

Reflected in concourse plate glass:
a grieved child in a nylon mask
putting her shoulder to the locked door.

4
The man's face is dark
as chocolate and his shirt
gleams grey and white like dirty snow.

Goya did not paint this.
But in Prado Room 32
The Third of May 1808:
tell me that is not the same face,
the same white shirt.

5
The kneeling man puts his weight
into it, crushes fermented
cacao beans, scrapes the nibs
into a tin bowl so luminous
it brightens my dim room.

Light is both wave
and particle.

6
To paint a word is to write.

To write is to paint a word.

I try to decipher the painted page
under the five cacao-pods.

It is a writ of manumission.
It's a love letter, *mi corazón*.
A foul paper from *Don Quixote*.

A copy of this poem
which has not yet been written.

7
O you eaters of chocolate!
How thoughtlessly you throw
the foil wrapper to your feet.
Do you not see how the kneeling man
has blistered his palms in labor
for your sweetness?

8
I hover over the museum
via video drone. I am in sky
and not in sky.

The man scraping chocolate
would never mistake a drone
for a blackbird.

9
Maize, potatoes, tobacco, tomatoes, cacao.
In Tenochtitlan Moctezuma serves Cortez
a golden goblet of *chocolatl*.

Later, the slaughter.

10
Beneath the pixels:
ten thousand lines of binary code
1s and 0s in precise and requisite order.

A simulacrum of a simulacrum.

11
In vain I look for the face
of the innominate painter
reflected in the lucent eye
of the man scraping chocolate.

A sunset reflected in a lake
is not in the lake.

12
I am eating chicken mole.
I am eating churros with chocolate.
I'm wearing a mask like my granddad did
for the 1918 Spanish Flu.

At the Book Fair author table
I scrawl my name
in a pristine first edition
encased in a mylar dust jacket.

13
The man is scraping
in the unsigned painting
and he will always scrape.

Askew, the blackbirds perch
in the stainless steel tree.

Mexican, Teotihuacan
Incensario

circa 200–600
Terracotta and paint
H. 16⅝ × W. 15⅝ × D. 10⅝ in.
Gift of Mr. and Mrs. John B. Fulling

Matthew Smith

Archaic Torso of Aphrodite

Rilke looked at a torso of Apollo
And heard the sentence *You must change your life.*
Profound advice, though difficult to follow:
Life has a way of reasserting life.

And if a broken god can still retain
His godlike powers and his godlike plans,
A man's life, no less fragile, no less vain,
Though changed for good will always be a man's.

Consider, then, this marble Aphrodite,
Still beautiful despite her missing parts,
Still recognizable as Aphrodite,
Still, even broken, fit for breaking hearts,

As if unchanged. And yet she seems to say
To you, who look too long, *Friend, look away.*

Greek, Attic, Leagros Group
Neck Amphora

circa 510–500 B.C.E.
Black-figure ceramic with
added red and white paint
H. 13½ × Diam. 9 in.
Purchased with funds from
the State of North Carolina

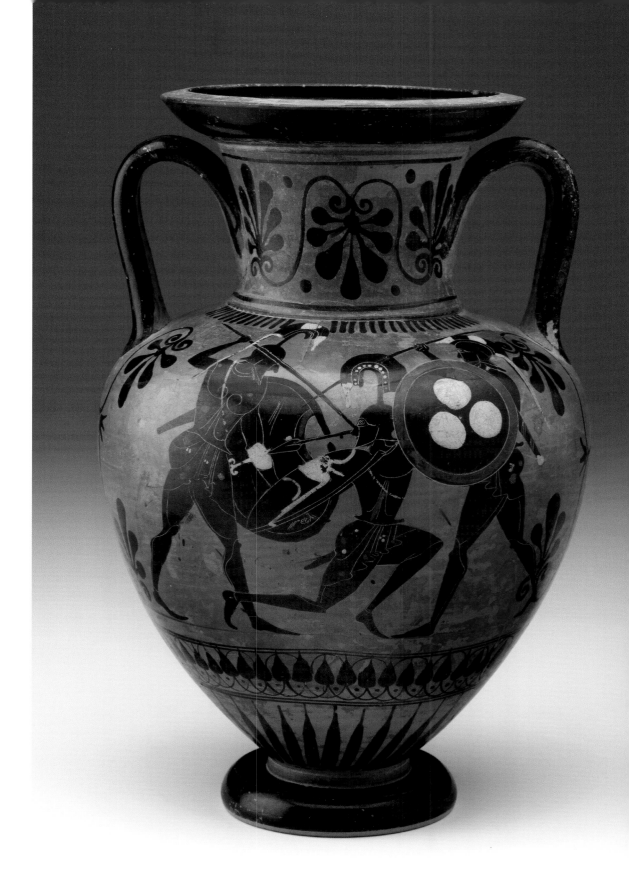

Alan Shapiro

On Men Weeping

1. MVP

He was The Man, he said—"Understand what I'm saying"—
out there tonight, The Man. So while his teammates capered,
hollered and whooped in victory's unembarrassable light,
he having done at last what he set out to do, his whole life
flexed for so long in the expectation he would do it,
having met the rigors of the challenge, the challenge's exactions
and observances, met and surpassed them each one in turn,
The Man, the superstar, was weeping as he raised the trophy,
weeping as he caressed it, kissed it, the taut face so finely chiseled
to a single purpose now a dishevelment of tears, the body's muscled
concentration gone, the body all limp with the release of it.

Weeping the way he wept, it seemed, was what he won for,
as if the trophy in his arms, in his swoon of touching, were
the glistening proof he'd now gone far enough into his manhood
to be able to go freely back in time before it, as if the prize
for having proved he was The Man was that he got to be the boy,
the baby, weeping the way Achilles must have wept
because he could weep now, the bronze gear recovered,
the degraded foe behind him dragged in a wake of dust,
the war car circling the dead friend's opulent pyre, foremost
among the grieving warriors, like a boy, a slave girl, weeping,
bloody, behind the massive shield that only he could lift.

2. The Family Face

My father had no prerogative of tears, not in the stark arena
of the rest of us, not after he had filed out with his sisters
from the back parlor sealed off like a privy where
the body of his father lay. Only there behind the door
the stone-faced courteous usher closed, stood guard before,
in the dim light that would have kept his face apologetically
half hidden even from his sisters circling the casket,
only there was he allowed to give in at last and wail
the way he hadn't since he was a child. Yes, only there.

For when they filed out past us toward the waiting cars,
only he could not stop crying, having given himself too
freely over to his keening to realize where he was now,
that he was back among us, so that his brother-in-law,
his sister's husband, Joe, the millionaire, the lord and
magistrate of what the family exacted, was obliged to say
in front of all of us, so all of us could hear, "Hey Harold,
cut it out, you're gonna set the girls off all over again."
And he did, immediately he cut it out, abashed, his hands

a moment covering his face, he choked back what he had
no right to, what he hadn't earned. For who was he after all?
What was he worth, the second son, the clerk, the diligent
but ever-struggling provider, with a wife who worked?
No way to lift the shield, no way to prove he could except
to recompose his face as a man's face, Joe's face, brittle,
cleansed of feeling—while Joe two decades later, even months
beyond her funeral, in front of everyone would sob for his wife
with all the inconsolable abandon that he had put away.

Guillermo Kuitca
People on Fire

1993
Acrylic and graphite on canvas
76¼ × 109⅞ in.
Purchased with funds from various donors, by exchange

Dorianne Laux

People on Fire

Kuitca's series *People on Fire* (1993) presents us with randomly
placed names in what might at first glance look like a genealogical
chart: anonymous names nonetheless, that have significance to
the viewer. These names, however, turn out to be the names of
people who have "disappeared," persons who were kidnapped or
murdered by paramilitary forces during the Argentinean dictator-
ship of the 1970s. —NCMA

If they were on fire we could find them, small human
flames lighting the night, flickering between trees,
tumbling down hillsides like the lit windows of houses
at suppertime, the smell of simmering, the sound
of laughter, the youngest ones sleeping nearby.

But they are gone, like a child in the supermarket
you turned your back on for only a moment, gone
like summer when the clouds move in, long trains
of shadow filled with boxcars of rain, gone up
in a puff of smoke from a cigarette thrown

out the back door and over the yard, caught
in the spider's web woven into the tree. Their faces
hovering below stars, their outstretched arms
and running legs making new constellations:
padre y madre, hermanos, abuela y abuelo,

gone to dust, gone from this world into another.
If they were on fire we could follow them
into the dark, into the burning bushes. God
give us water and angel's wings, a river, a well,
anything but this emptiness that has no mouth.

Egyptian
Model of a Boat

circa 2181–1880 B.C.E.
Wood with gesso, paint, and twine
H. 30½ × W. 20½ × D. 41 in.
Gift of Mr. and Mrs. Gordon Hanes

Mildred Kiconco Barya

A Life in Fragments (of a Boat)

Fragment I

More than any other means of transportation, perhaps, a boat makes you aware of your past, present, and future. When you sit on it, you don't merely think of where you are going. It is easy to remember where you are, the reason you are travelling, and how you might return. It might be the slow start that brings your entire life into perspective, or the waves that make you ponder matters of safety, relief, and creatures that could be lurking in the waters. In an airplane, if you enjoy flying, you may only focus on being in the present moment, exhilarated. If you're afraid, again, you do not abandon fear until the plane lands. In a car you are often attending to where you need to be, so the movement in both the vehicle and passenger is forward. The train, well, the train comes close to the boat.

Fragment II

In ancient Egyptian belief systems, the sun god Re travels in a boat through the netherworld, from the moment he dies after setting in the west, to the time he's reborn at sunrise in the east. In the depth of the dark, the sun's return to life is ensured after uniting with the mummified corpse of Osiris— god of the dead. It's this mystical union of life and death that binds all living things, and in which we find renewal. For the sun god's journey to succeed, however, it must be protected by qualified guardians, who are themselves deities, and other beings of integrity, thus charged with ethical responsibility. You see, the sun god has some enemies, the most terrifying being the demon Apopis—also called Apep—the incarnation of evil, who uses his dark powers to transform into a great serpent or dragon. Apopis hates all life and desires to annihilate the cosmos.

Fragment III

The sideways rocking of a boat amidst pauses and the expanse of the water, as well as the intensity of the current, all contribute to making one's thoughts, emotions, and memories, change rapidly. The boat serves as a model of reflection, internalization, and externalization of what's inside or outside, even beyond time and space.

Fragment IV

I am told that the sun god, in all his glory, power, and splendor, cannot look directly at Apopis without turning blind and falling into the abyss of nonbeing. Imagine what our own life on earth would come to without the sun. So it goes that in the sun god's darkest hour, Re swallows his light as Apopis rises from the underworld, ready for the kill. Seth, aka shadow, who once murdered his brother Osiris, is the only one known to look evil in the eye and survive, because he carries the same dark principle as an impulsive, violent, and chaotic male. The difference, however, is that Seth loves life. While he embodies destruction and intense, instinctual urges, he's also blessed with healing and creation. So he joins the sun god's crew, and you can see him standing at the prow of the boat determined to confront Apopis. Seth is aided by Isis, one of the two ladies rowing the barque, and also known for her fierce, militant spirit, love, and magical mastery. Apopis has no chance to win. The continuity of the sun's consciousness and regeneration are assured beyond death—the afterlife. Every night, the cycle repeats.

Fragment V

To be ferried—whether you're a sun god, goddess, or mere mortal—you must trust the team rowing the boat, give up control, and allow yourself to be carried. The virtues of teamwork, cooperation, faith, and hope are involved. We may not mention love, but it's in the service as well. And gender balance. The boat is about character and the soul of beings. It requires souls to be light. The hearts are weighed and, if found wanting, no protection or safe passage can be offered. To join this boat, one needs music, gladness, food, wine, and other forms of merriment that convey cheerfulness. This cannot be shallow, for the deities can see through.

Fragment VI

Blacks were captured from the hinterlands and shores of Africa and brought to North America in boats UNLIKE this. Theirs spoke of absolute horror and the most inhumane suffering that defies understanding. There were no rescuers, but rather extinguishers of light. The Blacks who survived the gruesome journey to this land, what can I say? Such grit, such strength, speaks volumes about the indomitable African spirit, and descendants of the ancient Egyptians. Perhaps they prayed to the sun god to remain alive, thinking that the ships would not go back after the loved ones they left behind. Those who hauled themselves into the bloodied waters, who gave themselves up to feed the sharks, I do not judge. I bless them all, along with the ones who died in slavery or by lynching, without Seth standing in-between their Apopis captors. Isis was not on this boat, nor was the vessel furnished with everything my brothers and sisters would need in their Middle Passage.

Fragment VII

Each time I see the sun, I think of the defenders of the barque who persist in their service. Each night I sleep, I pray the world does not plunge into dissolution. In my dark night of the soul, I think of the boats that anchor my life and ferry me from trouble. I don't see the sun in the boat but rather, what appears to be a mummified figure of a man, woman, or child. Dead outside, alive inside, and sometimes the other way round. Once in a while I wait for the boat, and wait, and wait. I don't always see the boat but blessed are the hours when it comes—help is on the way.

Marsden Hartley
Indian Fantasy

1914
Oil on canvas
46 11/16 × 39 5/16 in.
Purchased with funds from the State of North Carolina

David Gessner

An Elemental Fantasy

THE BLACK THICK OUTLINES around bodies and faces and fish. The square-shouldered square-headed men on the docks with their lobster pots and lines. The people-less paintings with the dashes of silver and white and chalky blue. Five mackerel lying on a table, the living blues and radiant whites of their dead bodies surrounded by those thick black lines. Lines that also surround the mountainscapes, rendering those loaf-like hills child-like but also somehow primal.

Primal. It is what we come to expect of the best paintings of Marsden Hartley. And it is what he found in painting itself. Despairing of where the world was heading, he sought the simple. If he did not read the words of his contemporary, Henry Beston, another cultured artist who wanted out of his culture, he certainly believed them: "The world to-day is sick to its thin blood for lack of elemental things, for fire before the hands, for water welling from the earth, for air, for the dear earth itself underfoot. In my world of beach and dunes these elemental presences lived and had their being, and under their arch there moved an incomparable pageant of nature and the year." That is the gift Hartley's best paintings give us: the pleasant shock of a return to a more elemental life.

Indian Fantasy is not one of his best paintings. Maybe it's the century that has passed since he created it that makes it seem a little like something a stoner teenager might hang on a dorm room wall. Maybe it's the stock Indians in headdresses in their mirrored canoes, or the giant non-eagle that looms over the teepee, or the teepee itself, that cause the painting to look, to my eyes, like a jumble of colors and cultures, the sort of composition that led none other than Georgia O'Keeffe to say of Hartley's work of this period that it was "like a brass band in a small closet." May-

be the mirror pattern itself is the problem. I don't come to Marsden Hartley for pattern. I don't come to him for neatness. Maybe this celebration of the so-called primitive isn't primitive enough. Where are the thick black lines that outline the lobsterman's face and arms, where is the startling simplicity?

Of course *primitivism* is a word that has rightly gone out of style. I am using it here, quite distinct from *primal*, in two ways. One is a description of an artistic style and method, the use of simple bold lines and archetypal patterns as opposed to anything complex and composed or overstylized (though brute simplicity is its own kind of style). But the second definition of primitivism is the one that holds a clue to how this work, painted in 1912 and one of six in Hartley's *Amerika* series, came to be. In her preceptive essay "Marsden Hartley's Native Amerika," Wanda M. Corn lays out the backstory. This is the work of an expatriate American alone in Berlin in a modern art world that has recently begun, led by Picasso and Braque, to celebrate the art of Africa, art in which it finds an authentic and simpler alternative to the increasingly industrial and dirty modern world. And, as Corn points out, Germany was a country that romanticized America's Indigenous people to the point of fetishism, devouring books and art about Indians. This meant that Hartley, in one fell swoop, could ride the tide of primitivism, currying the favor of the art world and, by substituting Native American culture for African, could also assert both his originality and his own nationalism. In other words, he might have been following his muse but creating the *Amerika* series also made sense.

The paintings don't. The three heavily patterned works that make up the *Amerika* series are a jumble of cultural appropriation. The particular painting I have been staring at for the last few days is, as the title suggests, a fantasy. Hartley didn't know anything about Native American peoples. He had never been West, had never met an American Indian, and didn't do any research. His "knowledge" came from movies and books, and it shows. His Indians are a mishmash of tribes from various climates and cultures. This was hardly unusual for an artist of his time. But it does provide something of a roadblock to appreciating it in ours.

Which brings me to the bird. Hovering over the entire painting, up atop the teepee, is a cartoon eagle staring us down while its pitchfork talons graze the teepee's top. Some critics, including Professor Corn, suggest that the eagle might symbolize Marsden Hartley himself since the beak-nosed artist was known in some circles as "the eagle of Maine." Corn also suggests that the eagle's power and ascendance might have reflected Hartley's own soaring mood at the moment as his paintings began to gain acceptance and he began to feel at home in the gay subculture of Berlin.

Often our personal reactions to paintings are a curious mix of the learned and the instinctive. What I find instructive, what fills out this painting for me, is the fact that Hartley had been corresponding with Kandinsky around the time he created *Indian Fantasy*. Hartley admitted his affinity for the Blue Rider school and it shows in his other paintings at the time, where the symbols, including Germany's iron cross, float more freely than they do in his rug-like tributes to Native peoples. And at that very moment Kandinsky was undergoing his own transformation. It was a transformation I witnessed retrospectively while strolling through a chronological display of Kandinsky's paintings at the Lenbachhaus Gallery in Munich. I was in my twenties at the time and doing some painting of my own, and I remember being terribly excited when Kandinsky's paintings first broke from realism, but then getting bored by the pure abstractions. It was an important aesthetic moment for me. I realized I like the exact point where something breaks into something else, when the horse breaks free from the barn. Things attenuate for me when they become too much one thing; they are healthier when becoming something else.

Hartley's eventual evolution was like Kandinsky in reverse. The colorful free-floating symbols of Berlin would constitute the first great surge of his career. But for me, it is only when he comes back across the Atlantic, returning to his native landscape of Maine and the people who work that landscape, that his work is truly great, truly elemental. I suppose it is more accurate to describe this part of his career as the horse in the process of returning to the barn, not breaking from it.

Having stared at *Indian Fantasy* for the better part of a week, having become that stoner teenager with this poster on my dorm room walls, I have grown fond of it. It takes some looking, and some empathy, but I have begun to see hints of the elemental work that he would one day achieve. The twinned campfires, one ash gray, the other orange-red. The simple pots and faceless fish. The vivid colors. The childlike almost consciously awkward depiction of the eagle. There are hints of what's to come, though you have to look hard. But we have an advantage, perched above his life in the present like the eagle: we know not just where he was but where he was going.

Master of San Jacopo a Mucciana
St. Jerome in His Study

circa 1390–1400
Tempera on panel, with gold leaf
35⅛ × 20⅛ in.
Gift of the Samuel H. Kress Foundation

Michael McFee

Portrait of the Poet
as Saint Jerome

No wonder I look miffed:
all I wanted to do today
was sit here at my desk
in a dazzling crimson robe

inking letters and words
on blank waiting pages,
surrounded by shelves
of books whispering *Write*.

Instead, that miniature lion
is bleeding on the carpet
near my dropped hat,
paw lifted in supplication,

Christ is exsanguinating
on a black cross outside,
His gaunt body ruining
my view of the world,

and the fallen-angel sun
of an ornate gold halo
makes my big head ache.
Must glory weigh so much?

Lord, all I'd hoped for
on this fine clear morning
was some time to myself
to put lines on paper,

to praise your creation
without such distractions:
no blood, no holy pressure,
just a few precious hours

when, if I'm lucky, my pen
and hand will synchronize,
translating the mysterious
into a common tongue—

what a miracle! I stretch,
then scratch my bad tonsure,
taking three deep breaths
before pronouncing *Amen*.

Gerard Seghers
The Denial of St. Peter

circa 1620–2
Oil on canvas
62 × 89½ in.
Purchased with funds from the State of North Carolina

David Brendan Hopes

Gerard Seghers: *The Denial of St. Peter*

Observe how every circumstance conspires
against the keeping of faith.
The eventful day sinks past its prime;
the dangers mount; the advantages dim;
the confused witness requires
the question to be put a second time;
in the mind's twilight a thin wraith
hovers, who was the once-beloved Him.

Observe how Peter turns away
from the golden, central light
to address his denial
to the dark periphery,
how hands uplift, how fingers splay
as if they were surprised this trial
would end so disappointingly, which might
have nailed a martyr to another tree.

The woman in the wrinkled turban
raises her finger to accuse.
I do not know him, cries Peter's right hand
gripping the astounded heart. The listeners lurch
to attitudes of disbelief, and yet again
I do not know him, says the left hand
raised in a mockery of blessing. This must amuse
those who heard Christ's, *Peter, build my church.*

Bald Peter in the mercy
of that triple lie excuses flagrant husband,
prodigals, false witnesses, amends cheating wife,
betraying friend, failed father, all the flood
of easy sins, the mortal heart's catastrophe.
Three times. After three cock crows comes life.
After three days the Pentecostal wind
transforms to rose the taint of blood.

Observe how none of this is shown.
In the next heartbeat the shabby fisherman
walks on till the soldiers' candles fail,
in darkness then,
a blackness outward from the bone,
a proverb of betrayal,
astonished, horrified.
Alone.

Workshop of Apollonio di Giovanni
The Triumph of Chastity

circa 1450–60
Tempera and gold leaf on panel
23 × 23¼ in.
Gift of the Samuel H. Kress Foundation

Kevin Boyle

Seed Pods and Chastity, 1458

I BOUGHT MY WIFE this lovely tray the week after she let me know she was with child, our first. I encouraged her to use the twelve-sided panel as if it were a clock face, reminding her to focus every hour on the boys playing with their seed pods—poppies, I was told—just beneath our family crests. One of the two naked boys held the seed pod close to his friend's groin, knowing the pod protects the seed to ensure new life. So too, my wife, would help her pregnancy come to term by looking at and thinking about the boys, the pods, their groins, and when the child was delivered it would be a boy. It would be a boy, the craftsman assured me. If my wife dutifully focused on the playful, naked, pod-wielding boys.

When Giacomo was born that May, I said a prayer of thanksgiving and quickly turned the tray over to show my wife in her postpartum gowns her new focus: while you nurse, while you sew, while you prepare your face and sip your broth, I would like you to look closely at the scene in which Cupid's wings are clipped and the perfect ladies, in groups of two or three, are part of a spotless procession. I would like you to think about how you can remain chaste while still loving me, how honor and modesty and purity can still be yours if you abstain from going beyond our bedroom walls. Never let your mind stray from this panel painting, this artful parade, this triumph of chastity led by the virginal unicorns.

That winter I returned the birth tray to the Florentine craftsman, explaining that despite the beautiful gold leaf, it was defective. Yes, our boy was born, but now I was without a true wife. I asked him to please remove the family crests and then he could do with it as he wished. "This is a donation," I said, and he took it and placed it inside a purple, twelve-sided cloth sleeve, never, perhaps, to be seen again.

Jan Miense Molenaer
The Dentist

1629
Oil on cradled panel
23⅛ × 31⁹⁄₁₆ in.
Purchased with funds from the State of North Carolina

Emilia Phillips

Extraction

But what of the tooth
in question? That absent root calcified by some
projection into bone turned molasses gunk
or, worse, a clang in my gum, its nerves strung
like piano guts & struck with one glance
at the aquiline pliers the dentist
steadies in the boy's mouth collapsing
past details' definition. What's supposedly rotten
never rendered. Unless it's palimpsest—
a smudge beneath the likeness of cream
in his cheek, its contortions deepened
by that Dutch shadow, the color of a whole
culture. The tooth for which the dentist sleuths
isn't there, just as the dentist's right ear
isn't there or the world outside
the window that lets in only a little
light. Which is to say, a different
color—something like pulverized
peaches in yogurt, which is probably all
the boy would be able to eat after
the dentist's through with him.
Which is to say, this dentist will never be
through: always in medias res, his gaze
always fastened on what he suspects
he needs to remove. Should I say, "Like a cop"?
Or should I turn, like some of you
other white poets, to the classical—
the bird returning again and again
for the liver? Did you know that it was called
"The Caucasian Eagle"? Now, on a highway

in America, I see a diesel
truck's rear window plastered
with an American flag
foregrounded by a bald eagle.
Even our national bird is white
on top, brown below. This is only
"a clever metaphor for identity
politics," some of the white poets
say. "Show, don't tell" is a way
to erase what someone
needs to say. Never say this
to another student, Emilia.
Never refer to the place
where no text lives as "white space."
Never forget that the great white art
is sustaining pain for centuries.
Every attempt you make to change
this trajectory will be flawed. Still
make it. Ask yourself every day
if you feel more of an ache
in your jaw, your nerve
lit like a line of gunpowder,
when you look at a four-hundred-year-old
painting of a white European dentist readying
to extract a tooth from a white European boy
than when you watch another video
you have no right to describe
here, no right to colonize.
Remember, Emilia, your best poem
is sometimes to step aside.

Kehinde Wiley
Judith and Holofernes

2012
Oil on linen
120 × 90 in.
Purchased with funds from
Mr. and Mrs. Gordon Hanes
in honor of Dr. Emily Farnham,
and with funds from Peggy
Guggenheim, by exchange

96

Sayantani Dasgupta

On Kehinde Wiley's *Judith and Holofernes*

IF YOU ARE AS UNFAMILIAR with biblical stories as I am—granted, I attended a Catholic school for twelve years, but because I grew up in New Delhi, my sense of iconography stems mostly from Hinduism, then Islam, then everything else—let me tell you about Judith and Holofernes.

On the orders of King Nebuchadnezzar, Holofernes, an Assyrian general, invades the Jewish city of Bethulia. He earns the wrath of a young widow, Judith, who swears to kill him and avenge her people. On the appointed day, Judith rises early. She prays, and dresses herself in fine clothes. She enters enemy camp, her mind set, and her eyes in search of Holofernes.

Judith possesses extraordinary beauty and charm. In no time, she catches Holofernes's attention. When he approaches her, he is already drunk. She encourages him to keep at it. Finally, when he is stupid drunk, when he can neither stand nor offer resistance, Judith grabs Holofernes's sword, and beheads him in one swoop, thus keeping her word to her people.

What happens to Judith after?

Some, glorify her strength. *Really, how did a young woman take on a mighty military commander on her own?* Others, praise her virtue. *Judith never took up with another man. After her husband died, she lived as a celibate for the rest of her life.* Yet others, praise her courage. *Judith was the heroine we needed, a true symbol of resistance against tyrants.*

Over and over, artists reimagine Judith.
Now she is blonde, and wears her straight hair in a neat bun.
Next she is brunette, and her unruly hair hangs down by her face.
Now she wears a gown of red velvet, and a jaunty hat with feathers.

Then she is nude, her breasts exposed, and her arms and shoulders muscular, like a man's.

Even Holofernes's sword does not remain a sword. In the hands and imaginations of various artists, it switches between a cutlass, a scimitar, a machete, and a saber.

It is impossible to look upon Kehinde Wiley's depiction and not notice his Judith's brown skin; her resolute chin and wide nose; the thick, black hair, lofty like a crown; her contemporary, off-the-shoulder, royal blue dress that she wears with a leather and metal belt; and the striking electric blue, yellow, green, and orange of the flowers in the background.

What's most different, however, is Wiley's Holofernes. A white woman. Who is she? A specific kind of voter? One of the two women who told me in the first week of my shiny-new position in North Carolina that "all jobs go to brown women these days?" Or perhaps it's not human at all, it's a mannequin, and by slicing off her plastic head, this Judith—perhaps the owner of a retail store in a fashionable nook of North Carolina, or a regular shopper like you and me—is announcing that she is done with conversations about the ideal body type in American, and increasingly, global fashion? That she is clearing house, and ready for change.

It's impossible for me, a Bengali Hindu, to not recognize biblical Judith's similarities to Kali. Though an atheist since fifteen, I remain socially and culturally rooted to the faith I was born into. I continue to be fascinated by the goddesses that make up the Hindu pantheon, and by all that they represent. The warriors Durga and Kali; Saraswati, the patron of art, education, and learning; Bhadra, the goddess of the hunt; Manasa, the mother of snakes—and the thousands of others whose names and attributes I have yet to learn.

Irrespective of the artist and the form of representation, Kali always appears with a weapon—a sword, a scimitar, or even a trident. Both her name—from the Sanskrit *kaal* meaning *Time*—and her dark skin, represent timelessness and infinity. She appears naked, with unruly, black hair, but because she exists beyond our realm, our concepts of good, bad, pure, impure, pride, and shame do not apply to her.

In her most ferocious avatar, Kali faces the demon Raktabija. His name, made up of two words, *rakta* (blood) and *bija* (seed)—literally means, "for whom each drop of blood is a seed." And indeed, for every drop of blood he sheds, a clone appears. He replicates himself, again and again, until he fills the battlefield with himself, thus overwhelming his opponents.

Until, Kali appears. She enlarges her tongue and spreads it wide to catch every drop of Raktabija's blood before it touches the ground. Then she expands her mouth and swallows his clones. Thus powerless, Raktabija finally meets his end.

Perhaps, Raktabija's blood represents our desires, and the battlefield, our restless mind. Kali is our reminder to live clutter-free, Marie Kondo style, because the moment one desire is met, our mind searches for another. Kali beseeches, *please stop. Will this new desire "spark joy?" What if it's ephemeral? Here now, gone the next?*

I wonder if Wiley's Judith, too, is delivering a similar message. *Look me in the eye*, she commands. *Watch my sword arc through air, and land right where it's supposed to. Don't be afraid. Look, there are flowers behind me, an entire Garden of Eden if you will, and I, a modern Eve, starting things anew.*

Roman

Head of a Woman in the Guise of a Goddess

1st century
Copper alloy and silver
H. 12½ × W. 8 × D. 8¾ in.
Purchased with funds from
the North Carolina State Art
Society (Robert F. Phifer
Bequest), the State of North
Carolina, and various donors,
by exchange

Jennifer Whitaker

Head of a Woman in the Guise of a Goddess

Begin bloody—or, so I assume: word-bound, I look for clues
in what they've called you, but where your name came from,
I don't even know: and where did the rest of your body go?
(Was there ever a body to be had?) (*To carry around the body
of a woman marks us.*)

We're used to the gods disguising themselves:
to toy with mortals, find an afternoon's plaything,
turn into a swan to rape a girl: whatever suits. But you?
You're guised to hide—enemies imagined or real, affairs
out of order, or just life spread out before you, a dull grave—
oh, but here I disguise you as me. My six-year-old asks,
what do you want your superpower to be?
Of course, invisibility.

I assume it'd begin with blood, like it always does,
but then I look at you, mottled brown and green,
not just bloodless but calm even, slightly amused.
Death drained you of your real colors: no, not *death*
because you never lived. They call it your *burial patina*—
the most poetic thing I can see: the color you take on after.
Sandy soil, sea burial: wherever you're left leaves its mark.

I leave the fruit to rot in its bowl, never clean beneath the beds,
hundreds of other domestic sins because my brain says
none of this matters once you're dead. At dinner one night,
I assume the placid look of one unconcerned with buying food,
the bills, relationships that fail, too much gin, the constant drum
of death death death. I'll take whatever I want. Have tantrums so huge
they storm the seas. Surly children? Just eat them up.
What are you staring at? This is me in the guise of a goddess.

And what a privilege it is to hide: to have a body
the size and color that lets you. Your real color's been lost to burial,
where my mortal mind can't help but insert *death*. One summer day
the car's hot as hell and my six-year-old tells me *I wish
I'd never been born.* My body freezes: the fear of that wish—
akin to courting death, but darker still, all of you not just *gone*
but never here, no body born or ever made,
no ventricles to pump your blood, no blood, no brain, no start.
I assume *here's proof:* he's inherited my distrust,
dark moods no drugs can touch, all the boring brooding,
but then I look back at him from the front seat, and he's just hot,
hot in his small body, so hot he can't imagine a world that's ever not.
What will you be when you grow up?
Bodiless.

Albert Bierstadt
Bridal Veil Falls, Yosemite

circa 1871–73
Oil on canvas
36⅛ × 26⅜ in.
Purchased with funds from
the North Carolina State Art
Society (Robert F. Phifer
Bequest) and various donors,
by exchange

Lee Zacharias

Albert Bierstadt, *Bridal Veil Falls, Yosemite*

I KNOW YOU BY YOUR LIGHT. In those paintings of the west, peaks jut from dark valleys, shadows pierced by evergreens, the Jeffrey pines, firs, and mountain hemlocks of the Sierra Nevada, the spruces of the Rockies, needled branches like shafts upon those arrows. In your work the eye must reach for a lofty horizon, for the apocalyptic light that is beyond any human's grasp. You painted the pastoral, but not a place at peace. The light is much too violent. And by the time you died, it was considered overblown, your vision "too romantic." Taste had flattened, and the brushstrokes you hid so carefully, as if your work might pretend to be the real thing, were unmasked. Art was no longer detail but impression, suggestion rather than intent, for despite the photographs you sometimes made to paint from later, your work was never just a record. It was not the west you saw, but the west you wished to present, a land made even more majestic by that light. You were a showman, but by the end your fame had faded, your manifest destiny turned obsolete. Only half a century later, when wilderness became fashionable once again, were your paintings dusted off and brought from storage. For you it was theater; now it is nostalgia. Your Yosemite was not a national park when you accompanied a government surveyor to sketch landscapes to paint in your studio back in New York. In your Yosemite there are no parking lots, no visitor centers, restrooms, campgrounds, or lodges, only two mule deer so dwarfed by all that rock they look like toys, little props you added to the lower left hand corner lest we miss the grand scale of your ambition.

But before reaching Yosemite, you had to cross the Rockies. Yours was the first recorded ascent of the mountain still named for you, which you sketched that year, 1863, along with neighboring Mount Evans, which you christened for your companion's wife, whom you would marry three years later, after her divorce. Perhaps you saw that tempest brewing, for in your painting *A Storm in the Rocky Mountains, Mt. Rosalie,* the sky turns the mountains black and jagged beneath its terrifying cloudburst of light, as if God himself were making an appearance, the mountain turned into a stone tablet: *Thou shalt not covet* ... You sketched Mount Rosalie on the spot, but I wonder: did the sketch include the storm, which you did not paint until 1866, the same year you and Rosalie took your vows?

And I wonder if *Bridal Veil Falls, Yosemite*, painted sometime between 1871 and 1873, is colored by your memory of that wedding. There are the witnesses, the tiny mule deer, the erect evergreens, tall in the valley foreground, a small fringe atop the cliff. White clouds, blue sky, no menace here, though the light is just as dazzling, its brightness just as fierce. Still, there is a softening, two deciduous trees among the boulders on the valley floor, the more distant one a filigree of branches, the other larger, closer to our eye, a leafy crown that bows, leaning like a guest hoping for a better view of the bride's gown. Or could this be any wedding? The world suffers no shortage of these nuptial falls after all. It's the obvious appellation. But who is this bride? Who designed her dress, and what unique features does that veil conceal—a plump mouth waiting for the groom's kiss or are the lips thin and tucked, set in resignation? And what of the light in her eyes, which are always turned away, her back to us? Is there a real person behind that veil? Or are the falls only more of your extravagant light, an illusion that cascades without end, trailing past any threshold we might see, a silky train the attendant rocks carry beyond the painting's gilt and ornate frame?

One criticism of your work is that it has no middle distance, but here a mist drifts outward, across the creek bed through the pines, the light itself a middle ground. And if there is an absence, isn't that just the nature of your subject? I know waterfalls, I have photographed them. At all but the most gradual of trickles, there is here and there is there, but there is no in-between. It's that lack of conjunction, the sheerness of the drop that draws us to them.

In the world there are forty-three Bridal Veil Falls, at least twenty-five of them in the United States. Of those last I have seen seven or eight, including yours in Yosemite, though my visit came on an August day more than a century after your painting, and the veil had thinned, grown flimsy with summer's drought. The mule deer were replaced by tourists scrambling about the rocks in bright T-shirts, guidebooks and cameras in hand, faces no doubt slathered with sunscreen. Who knows what SPF works best for the sublime? My visit was on an ordinary sunlit day, bright but lacking drama, the scenery spectacular but unsanctified by your beatific golden vision. In Telluride I drove a rented Dodge Aspen up a steep dirt road to reach Ajax Peak, grateful for the sedan's automatic transmission at every switchback, for even though it kept stalling out with vapor lock, had I been driving my own stick shift I would have surely rolled off the cliff. I intended to view this Bridal Veil Falls from the crown, but when I got there two men on motorcycles pulled up and pointed to the dusty brownish-gold Dodge. Did I drive up the mountain in *that*? "I sure did," I said. Never mind that had I lost my nerve, there would have been no place to turn around. I had achieved the near impossible, why shouldn't I be proud? They shook their heads. "You stupid bitch," they said and peeled away. I had the summit to myself, but the light was from the wrong direction, and if I took any pictures, they are lost.

In Ohio I drove in circles looking for the Bridal Veil Falls in spread-out Cuyahoga Valley National Park, but when I found them, the viewing platform was off to the side, so overgrown with trees there wasn't a clear shot. At Bridal Veil Falls in North Carolina's DuPont Forest, I bled all over myself for no reason I could see, clutching a tissue to the middle finger of my right hand, which had begun to seep from beneath the cuticle as soon as I started down the trail. There was no wound, but the blood would not stop, and it turned my tripod so slippery I closed it up and limped back to the ranger station for a Band-Aid—limped because a bone fusion the previous spring had failed and I was no longer a young woman who could negotiate an off-road trail in a rented two-wheel drive or scale a mountain on foot. I'd been sprier just a few years before, in Oregon, where I ran up and down the trail to find the best vantage point to photograph the Columbia River Gorge's Bride, because my husband was waiting and it takes time to set up a proper shot, one that does not freeze the falls into

individual droplets but creates instead the silk-white veil. A snapshot halts a waterfall in its tracks; only a long exposure allows it to flow. Though the eye sees the illusion at a glance, the camera does not. From the excursion boat at Pictured Rocks National Lakeshore on the Upper Peninsula of Michigan, exposures are necessarily short, and I had less than a moment to jockey my position to crop the other passengers and their cell phones from my frame as the captain turned around, the falls being both the destination and midpoint of our tour, one of those commercial nods to nature's wonders—you've-seen-it-now-let's-go.

But did I see the Bridal Veil Falls in Rocky Mountain National Park the year that my friend Doris Betts and I headed up Fall River Road in our rented Camaro? I can't remember. Would Doris? I can't ask. She died several years ago. One website suggests, yes, we would have, they are near the road's beginning, but the map I bring up on another shows them at the end of a long hike. We would have seen Chasm Falls, though I have no pictures of those either. The only pictures from that day are of us, tumbling from the car, two writers from North Carolina on a holiday weekend from the conference we are teaching at in Denver, laughing because it's the Fourth of July and here we are in shorts holding out our arms to catch the snow.

I was a child when I saw my first Bridal Veil Falls, though in the old black-and-white snapshot taken on the American side of Niagara Falls I can't distinguish it from the other two. What I remember is the roar and the spray that rose around our faces even there at the top, at the overlook we visited far more briefly than my mother would have wished. Not until she was both retired and divorced would she see Niagara again and get to ride *The Maid of the Mist*. My father, who had little patience for her pleasures, had stopped only reluctantly for the overlook and vetoed the boat. The two of them wed in wartime and she wore a gray suit, which seems appropriate for the long skirmish of their marriage. She sewed what may have been the dream gown and veil hard times denied her for my doll, the very doll that I am clutching in the single other snapshot from that trip—me, my doll, and my baby brother standing in the grass at a rest stop in Ohio. This was long before Ken came along and my doll was no Barbie, just a girl sans mascara, big hair, and uplifted breasts, a girl as young as I was, too young to be a bride, too young to have any memory of that trip at all, only those two pictures and my mother's sullen story.

But your light? I would remember that if I had seen it at any of those falls. It was sunny in California and Telluride, overcast in Oregon and DuPont Forest, and the view in Ohio offered

such a poor angle I don't remember whether it was sunny or not.
If you want to photograph a waterfall, cloud cover or light rain
make for the best shots. Only painting allows for the apocalypse,
that hyperbole of light that is so beautiful and terrible at once.
Even unseen, there is an edge of vengeance in the sublime. Its
power splits the sky, just as the groom will split the bride. We all
know the symbolism here. The landscape is a ceremony and every
ceremony a ritual that hides the everyday truth. It has no room for
the slip of a car's heartbeat, bleeding fingers, malfusion of bones,
the bitter stitching of a doll's dress, or anything else that speaks
of being mortal. Every painting is a still life, forever bound inside
its frame. A fruit uneaten, a carcass that will never rot.

   I want to say no. The grape will sour, the flesh will fester.
No to your grand vision, for everything it fails to forebode, the
parking lots, the losses, the human disappointments. I want to
tear away the veil and show the bride for who she really is, turn
down your blinding light, and yank that curtain back, expose the
wizard with his bald patch, his cracked rose-colored glasses, and
his mismatched socks. But the word will not form, my tongue
is rooted in my throat, I cannot turn away. I am breathless here at
the foot of *Bridal Veil Falls, Yosemite*, transfixed by its hallelujah,
stricken by its glory, as awed as you intended, persuaded by your
shrine, mute witness to a measure that does not include me,
while outside the temple, the veil keeps falling, falling, falling.

Tom Hunter
Lover Set on Fire in Bed,
from the *Living in Hell
and Other Stories* series

2003
Cibachrome print
60 × 47⅞ in.
Gift of Lawrence J. Wheeler
and Donald Doskey

John Kessel

Lover Set on Fire in Bed

She'd been reading her copy of *Pale Fire*,
Bobby asleep beside her, when,
marking her place with the ribbon
that had wrapped his Christmas present to her
(a peignoir from Victoria's Secret),
she set the book beside her mug of Jack Daniels
and the photo of her mother as a bride
and got out of bed.

                She'd felt tired but not sleepy,
cold, so she put on her fur stole. Bobby didn't stir.
Still chilly, she got the idea
that setting him on fire might warm her.

Her pillow still bears the impress of her head.
The bedclothes thrown back on her side
are not burning yet. Many nights
they'd made love on this bed:
at one time he'd been hot for her.
Not so much anymore,
nor she for him. From the signs of
his indifferent breathing and closed eyes
he's not feeling the heat now, either.

On the wall above her head hangs a lithograph
of the Archangel Michael vanquishing Lucifer.
Michael raises a sword in his right hand
and holds the scales of justice in his left.
Lucifer cowers from one, or the other, or both.
Until recently the most beautiful of all angels,
though not yet banished from Heaven's pleasant landscape,
he's now turned bat-winged demon,
falling toward the hellish flames
that await in the corner of the frame.

Pierre-Jacques Volaire
The Eruption of Mt. Vesuvius

1777
Oil on canvas
53⅛ × 89 in.
Purchased with funds from the Alcy C. Kendrick Bequest
and the State of North Carolina, by exchange

Michael Parker

Vesuvius: An Aria

In San Francisco on the night of 17 April 1906 ... Caruso had sung a graceful Don José and returned jovially to the Palace Hotel ... At 5:13 a.m. the hotel rocked ... His bed wobbled, then tilted over ... Caruso was anxious to make a detour for the Opera House and salvage his costumes, but someone reminded him that it was already ringed by smouldering fires. He looked blankly at the speaker and muttered "Vesuvius" ... "It's Vesuvius," he kept repeating.
—from *Caruso* by Stanley Jackson

HE SANG THE WORDS first in sleep, when the pleasant tinkling of the chandelier above his bed crescendoed into dissonance, before the fixture was plucked from its mount and the ceiling sleeted glass. Then the bed began to shake and the tenor, accustomed to transatlantic ship-sleep, swam up from a dream in which he was crossing the water to his own beautiful country. Thrashing through water tinted orange by a fiery sky, he opened his eyes and watched a pair of boots heel-dance in through the thrown-open door of his suite. He understood then: he was still in California, and as the hotel began to sway, he added San Francisco to the list of cities where he'd never sing again. Pelted with chunks of ceiling, tossed to the floor by the last and most powerful ten seconds of tremor, Caruso closed his mouth tightly, tasted the chalky plaster dust, the metallic bite of blood. Seconds of stillness followed, like the slight but radiant delay after a note nailed high and clean turns an audience to stone. And then applause: window shades flapping, church bells tolling, one high horse neigh touching off a chorus of croupy dog barks and finally the crash of the first weakened buildings followed by the thunderous orchestra that roused him from the debris and sent him to the window where, facing the bay which reminded him of his home, Caruso opened his mouth wide to sing.

Notes not heard. An aria in only two words, backed by shriek and scream, earth rumble and ember spit. *It's Vesuvius.* He sang what he saw and what he saw brought sight: the familiar mountain exploding above the harbor, ash dappling the sidewalks in front of the *café-chantants* where he'd first sung in public. Naples beneath the blazing light: nocturnal sparkle of the gently curving bay, narrow twisting streets, harmony of hill and sea. He sang its beauty in a night lit by terror, sang ship riggings backlit by moonlight, sang moonlight strained through rain cloud. He set longboats asail with his song, sang them through rolling seas toward ships anchored in the harbor. He sang crazed streets, bridges teeming with all the people he wanted to save, people from life, from song. Beneath *Vesuvius* he sang his neighbors out from those dank tenements where he had grown up eating black bread and beans, sang from the grave childhood friends who'd died of malaria and typhoid. Sang herds toward the bridges past posts carved into busts of San Gennaro, patron saint of Naples, whose likeness the fearful flashed like shields at vengeful *Vesuvius*; he sang rats and cocks and foamy-mouthed dogs, men trampled by hooves of horses, sang it all in a voice which hours before on stage had emerged as sharp as California light but seeped from him now as thick and hot as lava.

He tried to sing what lay below: buildings folding into themselves like the slammed-shut covers of books, bricks and timber burying alive lovers. In a note held high above a trembling city, he scoured ruins for the woman who hours earlier had shared his bed, sang his way to where her breasts and bloodied kneecap peeked through plaster but found his words powerless to save her *Vesuvius* sweet tenor sifting dust from her left eye which stayed open, unblinking, defiant, a corpse's eternal gaze which became the moon above the city where ash rained, lava lashed the outskirts. *It's Vesuvius.* Beneath the bay his notes rose in bubbles, up through the water which had made his voice so clear and strong *It's* countless childhood hours spent diving from the Molo into the cool green water, floating up from the depths off of St. Lucia to glimpse, just before he broke the surface, cloud-tipped *Vesuvius its* sides raked with vineyards, pulling him into the delicious air, drawing from his lungs a voice erupting above a burning city.

 It's Vesuvius. From deep within came the rain of cinders that buried Pompeii, and from someplace deeper, ancient, untapped, rose the thickly vibratoed mudflow that covered Herculaneum. He sang an elegy for those claimed by the volcano only days before, while he was en route to San Francisco; sang elegies for the dead of 79, 1631, 1767. Song of lovers, of love triangles: Carmen, Escamillo, Don José; Sir William Hamilton, Admiral Nelson, Lady Emma; San Francisco, Naples, Caruso. *It's* the song of painters who set up their easels on the outskirts of the city and made *Vesuvius* their lifelong subject *It's* the song of the mountain boiling from its center, spewing words toward heaven *Vesuvius* rivulets of fire etched down its slopes, edge of the city buried in hot notes, *It's Vesuvius* exploding in music never heard *it's* a song unsurpassed until that morning years later when Caruso's last notes covered the sidewalks in ash, along the volcano-shadowed avenue, beneath the hotel *Vesuvio.*

Thomas Moran
"Fiercely the red sun descending / Burned his way along the heavens"

1875–76
Oil on canvas
33⅜ × 50 in.
Purchased with funds from the North Carolina State Art Society
(Robert F. Phifer Bequest)

Nicole Stockburger

Wind

Old trick of gulping a finger to test the direction
of the wind, how quickly you make the land disappear,

do away with place altogether. All I see is a mound of wet cloth
in summer heat, murder of pitch-black crows

standing in a field I can't name.
The sounds soaked with so many tongues calling for rain.

Evenings, you look to where the clouds form.
(You can't see what's right in front of you.)

Scratch out the South the way a woodpecker collects scars
while its prey remains hidden,

as if to say somebody will always be broken into by these images,
left out in the storm, but water

could never replace you touching me
the way I truly want it. In the middle of nowhere, we wipe

the dust off. Your blood on the counter
and I didn't stop it. Never having gone that far,

I saw my hands against your body's seams (and their colors)
and I was back home, where my father chopped a snake in two

with a shovel. No one spoke a word while he downed another beer. Shook
or writhed or collapsed out in the yard. Dandelion-smelling soap

in my mouth. The other kids made us do things
we didn't want to do in the trees. The whole world was still.

Crickets sounding their fires in the open window,
calling me to come to the sill

while the wind picked up, rushing through the branches,
through anything down there that moved.

Vollis Simpson
Wind Machine

2002
Steel and other media
H. 30 × W. 30 × D. 15 ft.
Commissioned by the North Carolina Museum of Art with funds from the William R. Roberson Jr. and Frances M. Roberson Endowed Fund for North Carolina Art

Alex Albright

Vollis and His Fun Machine

I want to make things that are fun to look at,
that have no propaganda value at all.
—Alexander Calder

Wheels were turning in my head and I had to get them out.
—Vollis Simpson

It's hard to describe this work or its reason for existence 30 feet
above rural Wilson County.
—Eddie Wooten

1. Wind works art, which dances with it a pirouette on a blue sky canvas or a dark one specked with stars or clouded over. Doesn't matter. No wind works it, too, with light (and all those reflectors!) and the angles it reflects, infinite. Stand beneath Vollis's fun machine and whichever way you look upon it, you'll see framed in the sky a kinetic new vision. On a still day, tilt your head and, still, it changes. Lose the wind you lose the grind and squeak, though still it's whole as if wind were not required.

But wind's what makes it fun, Vollis said: *Well, it's got a little whizzy sound to them and you hear a little who-o-o-o ... I hang some chimes under them so they'll make a little music once in a while. It sounds like a piano player, when I had them in mint condition.*

2. "Them" is the collection of mammoth whirligigs that Vollis Simpson constructed at his home between the Wilson County communities of Lucama and Rock Ridge, where Willing Worker Road dips down to Wiggins Mill Road and where, once upon a time, pasture and pond, woods and swamp, ditchbank and road, all were filled with flash and groan. After his first one attracted so much attention, Simpson began making more 'gigs on weekends and as he created a bigger and bigger stir, locally and on the international art scene, he made more more elaborately and then more. The tallest, at sixty feet, has 2,000 reflectors; the heaviest, 13,000 pounds.

Why? *Most of the time, my sculptures are about where I've been. I love airplanes, so there's a lot of them, and farm equipment and animals. It's mainly my history. I've done a lot of stuff in my life and I just wanted to do something odd, something people could enjoy and for the children. They bring their little pads and their little notebooks and their little pencils, and I let them sit out there and draw. And I'll go get them some candy. [When] I know they're coming I'll send my wife to Wal-Mart and get a sack full of blow gum candy and pass them all out. [Sometimes the schools] bring a busload down here and stay two or three hours. And sometimes they'll bring their lunch and I'll let them have a little picnic out there. It's fun to see them enjoy themselves.*

3. *I'm Vollis Simpson. I was born and raised at Old Hog Place place.*

Born in 1919, Vollis was one of twelve children. He was a perfect-attendance kind of student at Lucama High School, where he was also president of the Young Tar Heel Farmers, and a 1938 graduate (a 2010 *New York Times* profile says he "graduated 11th grade," which, in his *Times* obituary, got translated to "high school dropout"; public schools in North Carolina then went only through eleven grades) and went to work on *his* father's farm, the one his father had farmed. One of their sidelines was house-and-barn moving, and Vollis seems always to have preferred working the moving parts of machines over digging dirt. Drafted in 1941, he served as a staff sergeant in the Army Air Force, stationed on Saipan and working memorably with B-29s, the largest airplanes in the world.

Vollis arrived at Saipan after the awful three-week battle (over 25,000 Japanese soldiers killed), a turning point in the Pacific war because it would mean secure air bases for the new B-29s that would then be within striking distance of Tokyo. But before the B-29s could come to Saipan, they needed a base, with the longest runways ever made. Vollis was among thirty-six North Carolina men commended by Brig. Gen. H. S. Hansell, Jr., commanding general of the 21st Bomber Command, for their expert and expeditious building, between August and October 1944, of Kobler Field on the southern end of Saipan. They "took up the unfamiliar task of airbase construction in addition to their regular duties," and in addition to their priority task of completing the two 8,500-foot runways was "the unusual assignment of building administrative and service facilities as well as living quarters."

A Japanese air attack on the base in November 1944 damaged several B-29s, and it may well have been from one of these that Vollis used parts, including propellers, to power a clothes washing machine for his base. Because dozens of Japanese soldiers had disappeared into the jungle instead of surrendering after the battle—the last Japanese on Saipan surrendered months after the war's conclusion—his base was also under constant threat, so he further honed his mechanical skills by constructing booby traps to protect against night raids.

We worked night and day with bombs dropping all around us. I didn't think I'd ever see Lucama again. I was just lucky, I reckon.

Back home, his marriage to Jean Barnes on January 20, 1947, was the first of dozens of Wilson *Daily Times* news notes from the Lucama and Rock Ridge communities that would detail the Simpsons' social life regularly through the 1980s: frequent visits with her family, housewarmings, weddings and baby showers, funerals, big Thanksgiving feasts, Vollis and brother Dewey to the 1947 National Air Races in Ohio, excursions to White Lake and Airlie Gardens, Vollis and Jean's children off to colleges. One front page photo of Jean Barnes Simpson accompanies a story about Governor Terry Sanford's tax proposals, quoting her: "I think it is hard enough for poor people to manage without taxing essentials. I think we are already taxed enough." Another shows Vollis comparing his famously large hands to those of girls on a Louisiana softball team (said the novelist Allan Gurganus: "I love shaking his hand. You put your hand on his, and it's like two catcher's mitts closing around"). The Simpsons were such respected fixtures in their community that obituaries for both Vollis and Jean's fathers were front page news.

In 1950, he and two brothers built the machine shop on Willing Worker Road from which he would work as a self-styled jack-of-all-trades until his death in 2013: *For 30 years we worked on all kinds of farm and tobacco machinery. We even built our own parts—worked on every kind of machinery: truck bodies, tobacco trucks, you name it. I also had a house-moving business. I learned a lot about balance and adapting machinery in all those years.*

His first wind-turbined devices were made for work, not fun—that Army washing machine and a home heating aid he made during the 1970s oil crisis. He moved that one from his home to his pond-side, where it became the basis for his first whirligig and soon began attracting local attention. In 1984, he told a Wilson reporter that he didn't have a name for the "contraption" he'd built from that heater, or "a reason for its existence." He called it *a mess*, and from it grew the collection that within a decade would become "Acid Park."

He also clearly liked the mess he had made and the attention it garnered, and as he eased into retirement, he filled his days more and more with building contraptions from what others didn't want. What he collected to use was too good to be thrown away, he said, not "junk," "industrial waste," or "abandoned industrial products": *When I built it, I didn't know anything about art. I still don't. Didn't call it nothing. Just go to the junkyard and see what I could get. Went by the iron man, the boat man, the timberman. Ran by every month. If they had no use for it, I took it.*

4. Bicycles, tricycles, and cars and their tires, rims, and parts, airplane tires, cones, metal headlight rims, scrap iron, reflectors, propellers, go-carts, hubcaps, road signs, HVAC fans of all sizes (Roger Manley noted his preference for "fans from barn [chicken-shed, pig-shed] ventilation systems—in both cases, unlike household fans, they could be super sturdy because you didn't have to worry about noise or the possibility of chopping fingers off"), ceiling fans, toasters, mirrors, stovepipes, I-beams, pipes, textile mill rollers, ball bearings, aluminum sheeting, various woods, steel rods and bars, rings, pans, milkshake mixers and cups, metal globes, heating oil drums, washing machines, metal wine goblets, roofing tacks, sirens, threaded rods and tie rods, and hundreds of cut-out figures from thick sheet metal, brightly painted stars, ducks, and farm animals were among his particular favorites.

5. I first heard of Vollis from my colleague Jim Barnes at East Carolina University, where I went in 1981 to teach freshman English. "Who knows about Acid Park?" became one of those ice breakers I'd ask at semester's start, like "Who's ever ridden in the trunk of a car?" or "Who's been crapped on by a bird?" Always a few students knew where it was, had been there, knew the story of how this man's daughter had died in an awful car wreck while tripping on LSD and he'd built this elaborate psychedelic memorial to her: you can even see the car she died in, with reflectors all over the trees around it and the one that's grown up in it.

After Jim left Greenville, I continued to stop by to visit Vollis, often bringing traveling friends to see what I had subsequently learned was one of two world-class Roadside America–kinds of attractions in eastern North Carolina—the other being Mrs. Way's Museum, in downtown Belhaven. Vollis was always generous with his time, sometimes working through a visit, and one-on-one always affable, though he'd rail against trespassers, litterers, and vandals who'd ride their four-wheelers through his nearby family cemetery, "overgrown but identifiable, with broken fence enclosure."

Once I asked him about the Acid Park story, and he leaned into the question with a sudden seriousness: *I never had a daughter killed in a wreck.* Not until much later would I realize the cruelty of this rural legend. The Simpsons' third child, their first daughter, had in fact died, not in a wreck but on the day she was born, in 1958, and she was buried in that family cemetery he so vigilantly guarded.

On another visit, he talked about trouble that had arisen when a booby trap attracted the sheriff's attention. He'd learned booby-trap making in the service, he explained, and the trip-wire worked, but his shotgun's birdshot load had been aimed too low, and one of the boy's trucks had been plinked. He agreed to dismantle the booby traps—(this may have been related to a February 1992 incident in which a charge of assault resulted in a voluntary dismissal)—which were sometimes also set to protect that cemetery. But the trouble didn't cease.

Reports of break-ins and thefts from his shop started in the mid-1960s, but they accelerated after media attention began attracting folks from farther away. It was three teenagers from Garner, an hour west, who triggered his arrest in 1998 on felony charges of assault with a deadly weapon with intent to kill, inflicting serious injury, and discharging a weapon into an occupied property. The indictment came two days after he was featured in *People* magazine.

The case dragged on for over a year, and the uproar over it brought letters of support to the local paper from artists and museums from all over the U.S. and Europe. Twice the local courtroom was filled beyond safe capacity with local supporters wondering why he'd been so charged when he'd been protecting his property after repeated acts of vandalism: his whirligigs used for target practice, bottles and bricks hurled at them—and him, once leaving his forehead gashed. The vandals, wrote one supporter, "deserve buckshot, not birdshot," and another argued that those "defacing and desecrating this beautiful spot" deserve the punishment. Had he been "intending to kill, as he is charged, he certainly would have used more powerful ammunition than birdshot."

In the end, Vollis pled guilty to reduced charges, a couple

of misdemeanors, and his thirty-day sentence was suspended. He paid for the emergency room visit two of the teens had made, and for the damages to the other's truck, and that one's dad dropped his civil suit against Vollis, who agreed not to have guns on his property for five years and to submit to warrantless searches for weapons.

6.

Only a few eastern North Carolina natives have their work included in the North Carolina Museum of Art's permanent collection. Wilmington's Claude Howell got accepted into his first juried show when Vollis was a high school junior and future farmer. Kinston's Henry Pearson drew maps for the Okinawa campaign, a couple thousand miles away from Vollis, in World War II; they'd both have gone to Hawaii for R&R. And Long Creek's Minnie Evans—how I love to imagine her working the gate at Airlie Gardens that day when the Simpsons came to visit, soon after the gardens opened in 1949, Vollis pausing to study her paintings. The Museum's spectacular 1989 show *Signs and Wonders: Outsider Art Inside North Carolina* brought his art to the attention of a worldwide audience, and the wrap-around photo by Roger Manley on the oversized catalog for that show is still the best static depiction of the site where it all began. These days, *Wind Machine*, which Vollis constructed especially for the Museum in 2002, looks a little lost in the landscape at the top of a lovely sculpture trail far removed from the five-points in rural Wilson County that used to be dominated by the most fanciful of personal parks.

Most of Vollis's fun machines have made the ten-mile move to Wilson, where they populate the Vollis Simpson Whirl-igig Park, and the site where they used to stand is ghostly quiet, like it had become as Simpson became unable to maintain their moving parts, and the mechanical symphony that permeated his environment was choked out by rust and vines that have now reclaimed almost all of what used to be his shop. One lone giant, safe inside an electric company chain link fence, still moves creak-ingly; the grass beneath it has been weed-eaten around its parts most recently shed. But still it works.

7. Heft and balance, air and color, shadow and shape, form within form, motion, mass (and massive). Geared: how one thing work-ing works another and it, another, *so long as the grease holds*.

Pause draws an arabesque.

What you see depends on time and place: how long you've got and when and where you stand to watch a constellation drawn with cutout stars and landfill gleans.

Paul Howard Manship
Diana

1925
Bronze with gilding
H. 63³⁄₁₆ × W. 42³⁄₄ × D. 17 in.
Gift of Ann and Jim Goodnight

Lauren Moseley

Diana

at first the goddess
of the woods and the chase
appears to have a tail

then I circle around and see
it's a scarf?
a sash?

I wish I could return
to when she was
prehensile

I wish I never learned
Diana cursed
an innocent man

or did she?
myths are stories
told by men

retold by Edith Hamilton
who even with her lifelong
female companion

blamed Diana
for punishing Actaeon
after he saw her bathing

now as I stand before
Manship's work
after the sash-tail

after the gravity-
defying breasts
what I see most clearly is

an amputation
Diana's missing
arrow

Claude Monet
The Seine at Giverny, Morning Mists

1897
Oil on canvas
35 × 36 in.
Purchased with funds from the Sarah Graham Kenan Foundation and
the North Carolina State Art Society (Robert F. Phifer Bequest)

Michael White

The Seine at Giverny

IN 1993, when my first poetry book, *The Island*, was accepted for publication by Copper Canyon Press, their noted book designer asked me what I'd like for a cover image. My first wife had died of cancer not long before, and I was still crushed. I'd taken emergency leave for two years to care for Jackie. Now I was back in Salt Lake City to finish my PhD at Utah. I could hardly deal with the designer's question. She sent me a big, fat art book to help me decide. I opened that book and almost immediately lighted upon *The Seine at Giverny* by Claude Monet. My first book is full of river imagery. *The Seine at Giverny* was a perfect fit. I called the designer and told her.

Here are some things I didn't know … I didn't know much about art. I didn't know that *The Seine at Giverny* was part of a series of about twenty known canvases (though I'm sure that the painting I chose was the one in the NCMA, because it's the only one in the series with such a delicate suffusion of violet and rose). I didn't know that Monet painted several other series like it in the 1890s. Or that, for *The Seine at Giverny*, he used a floating boat-studio—an old trick for him—moving quickly from one canvas to the next as the sun came up each dawn. I didn't know yet that violet (my favorite color) was the de facto color of impressionism, named after Monet's *Impression, Sunrise* (1872), which inaugurated the movement.

All I knew was that *The Seine at Giverny*, even in repro-duction, leapt off the page, addressing me with a clarity and urgency I'd never felt before. I think this had something to do with growing up in Missouri, very close to the Missouri River. It all came flooding back: I felt the force of current sweeping past me, beneath the deceptively flat and silvery surface. I smelled the silted water; I could feel its breath waft cool against my skin. After a few days, the designer called back and told me she'd thought it over. "Monet's too famous," she said. She'd seen enough books with Monets on their covers. My second choice was a gorgeous, lilac-and-yellow Théo Van Rysselberghe. I love it but still wish I'd lobbied harder for *The Seine at Giverny*.

What's so special about *The Seine at Giverny*? On the most basic level, the canvases in this series are square, which subliminally sets the subject matter apart: it's neither portrait nor landscape. There's also a device present that becomes increasingly rare in the other late Monets (absent, for instance, in the water lily paintings): a horizon line.

Except it isn't really a horizon line. We can't see that far. All we see is the far bank of the river, and the smoke-like, inchoate shapes of the trees above, bathed in pearlescent haze. This, I think, is the source of the delicacy. The line of the riverbank creates two worlds: my gaze flicks back and forth between the serene and hazy dawn above, and its glassy reflection, glimmering below. I can't choose between these worlds.

Because I've written a lot about Vermeer, I gravitate instinctively to him when I think about optics and painting. It wouldn't be fair to say that Vermeer paints only what can be seen. It might be fairer to say that his painting breaks down the process of seeing itself. We're faced with light meeting skin, in the moment of beholding, as if for the first time in our lives. Similarly, it wouldn't be fair to say that Monet paints only what can't be seen. It might be fairer to say that he breaks down the process of unseeing itself. We peer through a shifting veil of light and mist that half obscures and half creates the world—as we've never seen it before. As the artist famously said (a year before beginning this series): "To me the motif is insignificant. What I want to reproduce is what lies between the motif and me."

In this case what lies between the motif and Monet is incorporeal, mostly reflections. The river bends toward the left, around a dense growth of overhanging trees that dominates half the canvas—which, though thinly and wetly painted, is the only passage in the painting that really approaches representation. One thing I remember loving then, in 1993, about this particular work is that there isn't a clear demarcation between these trees and their wraith-like, emerald-green reflections splaying toward us ... There is no seam between the reality and the dream.

The second thing I remember loving then is the exquisite tension between abstraction and observation. The other side of the river consists of great, blurry splotches of pale violet and green washes—banks of trees that loom against the sky and that also, in reflection, stretch toward us, across the bend in the river, with no attempt made to blend or refine the pigment or the shapes. The abstract treatment, present here and especially in the water lily paintings, was the root of expressionism later—Pollock and company.

But there's something, too, about the way white brushstrokes cross the watery expanse in the right foreground—just the quickest possible touches of unmixed white, at slightly different angles here and there. There's something in the way they almost alchemically embody two seemingly disparate ideals. For these touches are pure mark-making at its freest and loosest, but at the same time seem spaced at just the right intervals to lovingly evoke—for those who have spent much time on rivers—the surface of an actual river with all its mysterious ripples and eddies.

I didn't think much about Monet in the middle of my life. Perhaps I, too, like the book designer, had started to think of him as too popular—a painter who belonged to virtually everyone, and therefore to no one. But in 2016, on my fourth trip to Paris, I had a free afternoon and finally made it to the Musée de l'Orangerie for the first time. Toward the end of his life, Monet staked all his bets on the lily ponds—which he had built a short distance from the scene depicted in *The Seine at Giverny*. By the time Monet was working on the Orangerie cycle of eight immense water lily scenes, he had lost his second wife; he was nearly completely blind; his work had fallen out of favor to the cubists; depression was ravaging him mercilessly. A frail Lear, locked in heroic effort, he lost himself in his lilies till he died. When I finally saw them, the immersive, hallucinatory visions in the two great oval rooms burned with Shakespearean splendor. I floated, utterly weightless. The notion that Monet could ever be too popular was suddenly absurd.

The Seine at Giverny enthralls in a much quieter way. It fascinates me especially for its refusal to settle either on the objective or on the subjective moment in time. It's both: it's one of the most convincing plein air scenes I have ever seen; and it's one of the most personal, too.

Here are a few more facts. In 1868, twenty-nine years before painting *The Seine at Giverny*, Monet tried to drown himself in this same river.

In 1994, thanks to my first book, I received a fellowship at Yaddo, the famous art colony in upstate New York. I spent the entire month of June trying to write about the tragic death by cancer of my first wife. Desperate for inspiration, I went to the nearby Skidmore College library, thumbed through a couple of big art books there, and found another Monet that burned a hole right through me the instant I saw it. It was his magisterial *Camille Monet sur son lit de mort*—his study of his first wife, just after she died of cancer. It opened a door. I could see my wife's face on her deathbed in the face of Camille Monet on her deathbed. The elegy that I wrote—titled after the painting and dedicated to my wife—was the only poem I wrote that month. It was my first attempt at ekphrastic writing, which became a specialty. I have since run into *Camille Monet sur son lit de mort* in five or six galleries around the world (its home is the Musée d'Orsay). I swear I can feel this painting radiate a singular energy across a room even before I see it. I'm never surprised. I turn a corner, and there it is.

After Yaddo, still in the summer of 1994, I accepted a job at UNC Wilmington and moved to North Carolina. I had no idea that my beloved *The Seine at Giverny* was here. I discovered this astounding fact at Christmas that year, when a new friend and colleague offered to take me to the NCMA. The painting waylaid me from the other end of a gallery. I could have fallen flat on my face.

That night, as we drove back to Wilmington, I remember trying to explain to my friend what *The Seine at Giverny* meant to me. I told her about growing up near the Missouri River, and I told her about the cover of my book ... I rambled on and on for hours. I should have just said, "it is my heart."

Pieter Aertsen
A Meat Stall with the Holy Family Giving Alms

1551
Oil on panel
45 ½ × 66 ½ in.
Purchased with funds from Wendell and Linda Murphy
and various donors, by exchange

Jonathan Farmer

To Pieter Aertsen, on *A Meat Stall with the Holy Family Giving Alms*, Written in the First Months of the Covid-19 Outbreak

Cast in oil, your timeworn irony
stays bright, its touch-screen transferred nearness real
as flesh skinned and exposed, still livid, still clean,
a butcher's bounty tumbling off the bier
of stall and table. That this survives is partly
fortune, partly skill, a nearer emblem
than those paintings of yours iconoclasts destroyed
to free the soul, of that vibrant, threshing whim
by which the earth is filled and cleared—of us.
But while the crossed fish point to Mary, paused
in Antwerp, somehow, smuggling her sacred trust
to Egypt, I don't much care. The humble cause,
ambered in your lavish present tense
and cloaked in your contemporary clothes,
is too remote. It's the gathering of sense
and being in that head stripped to the nose,
its eye alert and almost straining to see
what once was you and now—for now—is me,
a minor writer shoaled too briefly on
a minor grief—that, Pieter, that's what speaks
most clearly, here, where I seek words and song
to force some purpose in this gaping ease
of plague time. So who cares, Pieter, if I don't
adore your painting on its terms? Not you.

Past your painting in the photos on my phone
are pictures that in the first few days I viewed
almost obsessively, afraid to let
the loss recede, though soon enough it did,
being only the death of a beloved pet—
of Hopkins: still soft, still sweet, but thinned, subdued.
The quarantine had started, so we sat
out in the parking lot, and he climbed,
as he had at the shelter, into my lap,
to rest. Later, inside, he's back in my arms.
My face is red and strained, and he looks weak:
drugged and sluggish, vacant and disarmed.
I'm not sure why I keep these. They're too bleak:
They still remind me how his head flopped down,
limp as a baby's, shockingly vulnerable,
when I lifted his body for one more look, and how
when I set him down to leave, the full
weight of his body seemed to rest on one
leg bent beneath him, and, afraid it would break,
I had to rearrange him, I had to run
his legs out to the side as if to make
him comfortable—while in these final photos,
still alive, he's draped, splayed, in a way
no cat would tolerate, his back legs posed
too far apart, his belly twisted and displayed
far too plainly, his head all droop and weight,
a front leg torqued across my arm and wrist.
Nothing to say that he was wonderful, Pieter.
He was wonderful, and now he doesn't exist.

George Cochran Lambdin
The Last Sleep

circa 1858
Oil on canvas
40 × 54¾ in.
Gift of Peter A. Vogt

Jill McCorkle

The Last Sleep

MARGARET KNEW when she opened her eyes and looked about that she was looking on the world for the last time. It was the heaviness she felt, heavy of eyelid and arms. The very air was heavy with dampness and the smell of roses, velvet petals and thorny wood. Someone had placed one in her hand but she let it fall to the side. Her hands were numb with sleep, *dark with sleep* she heard someone whisper in passing. *The shadow is passing,* one said, *the time has come.* There were whispers throughout the days and nights, how much time had passed she did not know; it seemed an eternity and all the while, everyone she had ever known came and passed through the room like ghosts, like shadows. They talked of her illness as if it were human, a form to lie waiting, watching and waiting to strike the right soul. They said, *God needs another angel in heaven,* and she willed her body to rise to its fullest to raise one arm high if only for a second. She wanted to say, *Get from my room, I am not up and dressed.* She wanted to say, *who do you think you are anyway? Preacher or teacher or old Mrs. Combs from the market? You have no right to see me this way.* She could feel the anger in her neck and face, mouth twisting as she pulled herself higher and higher, high enough to see Charles at the door letting in more women with trays and jugs and boxes. She could smell chicken and biscuits, cheese and johnnycakes. *Get up* was all she could manage. *Nonsense,* she thought as she fell back against the pillow, someone there with a cool cloth on her forehead. This was a daughter's job. But she had no daughter. A son should have guarded the door, protected her, but she had no son.

She turned her head to the side, and beyond the people and the heaviness of the dark warm room she could see light. The dining room beckoned her, there, the chair by the window, the light making the room golden and hazy as in a dream. That was a healthy room. Every morning for ten years, every morning since she married Charles, a man old enough to be her father, and he brought her here to this house, she had risen early and sat there in the early morning light. She liked a moment to look out on the world before the work began. She liked to look out on their yard, a line of pecan trees flanking each side of the road up to the house. The land was flat and wide, pine trees filling in the spaces, their soft needles cushioning the sound of a walk into the woods. She liked to pretend that she was the daughter of the house, a princess trapped and waiting for something to happen, for somebody to come and carry her off to the seaside, a day's wagon ride away.

"Come quick," someone said. "She was trying to get up."

"She moved?"

"She spoke?"

"She said, 'Get up.'"

"Now, now, you got to stay put." Of all the voices, she knew this was Charles; too loud and too flat. He was forever telling her what to do.

A calm low voice came from the corner behind her head. She had heard this voice from the pulpit. She had heard this voice speak of God's anger at those who had fallen by the wayside. Those who walked through the world coveting and desiring earthly belongings and pleasures. She spent her whole childhood wanting her Aunt Emily's coat with the fox collar. Her Uncle William had shot the fox himself. Shot it and skinned it for his wife to drape proudly around her neck while her stomach got big and round and hard with what they would all soon come to call Helena. Margaret remembered being seven when she hid in the wardrobe in her parents' room while Emily and William were there visiting; she pulled that fox fur up to her face and felt the silkiness. Margaret wanted that coat. She wanted to grow up and look just like Emily with painted-up lips and red in her cheeks. Emily said that she liked this coat but what she really wanted some day was mink, and not just a collar but a full-length coat.

"You'd die in this heat, woman," William said, and they all laughed while Margaret squatted there and peeped out of the wardrobe. Later her momma asked who did Miss Emily think she was, royalty? Her momma said Emily had herself a bed with curtains draped around it like she might be Sheba. Margaret wanted that bed; she coveted that bed and when all was said and done she got it because nobody else wanted it. She was lying in it now like a queen. Margaret's parents talked of how Emily's daddy made a killing after the war. Textiles. Margaret's daddy said that only in these parts could a stupid man have done so well. Margaret wanted all that Emily had and when Helena was born she hated her at first, hated that Helena got to snuggle up to sweet-smelling Emily in that big royal bed. She often came and stood closely as Emily held Helena. She would reach her arms out to touch Emily, to stroke her long hair. Sometimes Emily let her brush it and she had to reach up high and then pull the brush through the long thick hair. Stroke after stroke.

"I have seen many reach out in such a way."

"Do you think that ...?" another asked, pausing for the divine intervention.

"The Lord works in mysterious ways."

"The Lord is my shepherd ..."

She closed her eyes against this recitation. This was her house, her church. If there was a recitation she would do it, thank you. The light would stay in the dining room all morning while she cooked the breakfast: sausage, eggs that she had just collected, fresh biscuits, milk, butter she had churned herself just days ago. She liked to sit on the porch with the churn at her feet and work the handle up and down while watching the road or the edge of the woods for a sign. If a redwing blackbird came and landed, for example, she might up and leave. It would be so easy to steal off across the yard, Charles busy out in the field, his body hidden by the mule and plow. Even if he glanced her way, she would head eastward and the sun would be so bright in his eyes that he would have to look away. He might think he saw her is all and he wouldn't know for sure until he came in for lunch and found his ham biscuits out on the table. She wouldn't even leave a note. She would simply disappear. It wouldn't be the first time that had happened, a woman up and disappearing.

If she chose to stay for one more day then she would find herself coming back to the dining room all morning just to catch the light. It would pass by early afternoon and then she would have the feather beds outside to beat and warm in the sun. She used a broom to beat and beat, each thwack striking a rhythm in her head. She would race through the yard to catch a chicken and when she got one she would snap its neck easily as a dried-up twig. She would bleed it and scald it; pluck it bald before rinsing and flouring and frying it up in fat. Used to she felt something for those chickens; she looked into their hard pebble eyes and begged their forgiveness for what she was about to do. She tried to swing them around in a gentle fashion but that was a cruel thing; slow death, neck only part broke. Would they race across the yard with no head as Charles said? She had no desire to know what a halfdead chicken might do. She would simply catch a chicken and ring its neck while looking elsewhere, thinking elsewhere; she would weed the garden, up and down, bending and stooping, reaching and pulling, her fingers running up and down pea hulls like a blind person reading the news. *Are they filled out? Are they ready?* She walked and walked, the sun high in the sky, her hair pulled off to one side, her face and neck drenched in sweat. Her basket was so full of peas she had to put it down, her hand and arm numb from holding it there close to her chest. She looked way out in the field where Charles was no more than a dot in her vision and she looked over at the woods, at the pine needle carpet. She could begin by walking and then set off running if she needed; she could make it into town and climb on the train. She could say she was going to visit some relatives; she could say she had somebody who was dying and who needed some help. Didn't dying people need all the help? Didn't they need all that food in there on the dining room table, piled so high it blocked her view? It was ruining her day and already the light was moving, shifting. Another hour and this side of the house would begin to cool while the sun baked the front, that afternoon light so strong and harsh. It made her close her eyes; it swaddled her with a numbness she could hear, buzzing like a head full of bees, a swarm of bees.

"Why her?" someone asked. "Too young," said another. She thought she heard her cousin Helena had died in childhood. She wanted to ask who in the room sounded like Helena. She wanted to ask now after all these years what exactly had happened to Helena because it was something she only knew as whispers among the grownups. "Helena?" she called, meaning what happened to Helena? One day she was out on the porch swinging her plump naked foot out into the summer air and the next she was stretched out on a tabletop for the neighbors to come and see, a still dead child with lilies on her chest. She meant to ask what had happened to Helena's mother, where was Emily on that very same day while William sat in the corner tying and untying his shoes—tying and untying—over and over like that was his vocation in life. "Helena?" she said again. She wanted the facts, but they misunderstood her request. They called her delirious; they said she was reaching for heaven, reaching for the light, reaching for the Lord Jesus to come and take her home. They said she was hearing voices, voices from a life that no longer existed. She was reaching for childhood friends and parents and relatives. But these people didn't even know Helena. They don't even know about all the days Margaret rose with the notion that this would be her last day spent alone in this house; her last day working like a slave to clean and cook. They don't know how she looked off into the woods and pictured herself there, running back to her childhood home, past the churchyard, past her school. It was tiring to run so hard, to work so hard, and her eyes felt heavy like she might close them just for a second. Charles was there now, his hand as rough as sandpaper against her face. The preacher was there, his breath tinged with the odor of the food he had been partaking in this very house. They all looked little to her. When they asked if she had any last things to say she was suddenly filled with the thought of all that she would *never* know. All that she would *never* do. There was no word for it all, no way to say it. So she closed her eyes to their tired old faces and let sleep come. When she woke she would be in a thick pine forest winding her way to the morning light. She would wear fox fur like a queen and she would never look back.

Nell Welliver
Breached Beaver Dam

1975
Oil on canvas
95¹⁵⁄₁₆ × 96⅛ in.
Gift of Lee and Dona Bronson in honor of Edwin Gill

Julie Funderburk

Walking into the Welliver

An inventory of sunlight and bark,
the woods thick with flashing birch.
Green deepens
where the beaver dam breached.
Where the forest has flooded
water is translucent as sky.
Such height in the shallows.
The trees extend
down into their own reaching,
a study of lines
hinged at the illusory plane.
Part of the story is an abandoned dam.
Part, a self-forgetting—
to follow the bent arrows
to mark the drowned
red-orange trunk
that absorbs my witness.

Thomas Hart Benton
Spring on the Missouri

1945
Oil and tempera on Masonite panel
30¼ × 40¼ in.
Purchased with funds from the State of North Carolina

Belle Boggs   *Spring on the Missouri*

IN EARLY 1937, it rained and rained across the American Midwest—nineteen inches, in some places, just in the month of January. When the *Kansas City Star* sent Thomas Hart Benton to sketch the catastrophic flooding across southern Missouri, he was struck by the movers he saw, and reported that "every once in a while seepage from under the levee would force evacuation of a house and you would see a great struggle to get animals and goods out of the rising water."

Spring on the Missouri grew out of one of the pencil and ink sketches he made for the newspaper: there are the same mules pulling a rickety cart, its wheels sinking into mud. There is the same crouched and hatted man, hauling goods into the cart. Dark clouds and driving rain threaten in the distance, where the flood has already surrounded another small house. The painting, completed in 1945, has a dramatic sense of movement that comes from additions of the imagination: a forked bolt of lightning; a second man, who helps lift a mattress into the cart; a blanket spilling over the side; an earthenware jug that will be left behind. The house in the painting is the solid object the movers and the flood work against: we see its brick chimney, the wood grain showing through the white, weather-beaten frame, the open window that no one will bother to close before fleeing.

Like some other populists, Benton was a bit of a phony—he'd come from a wealthy, connected family that had little to do with the mountain hollers he liked to ramble through or the ordinary people he liked to paint. His great-uncle, a senator, dueled with Andrew Jackson and almost killed him. His father, a congressman and wealthy lawyer, didn't want him to be an artist. Benton studied in Paris and at the Art Institute of Chicago before learning the harmonica and leading a bluegrass band in Greenwich Village. He was friends with Alfred Stieglitz, and was one of Jackson Pollock's teachers. But he was also a contrarian, an egotist, and an ideologue. By 1935, when he returned to Missouri, he'd renounced his friends, Marxism, modernism, abstraction, homosexuals, and the City. He said that New York had "lost its masculinity," and he continued painting in his somewhat garish, realist style.

At the moment I cannot see *Spring on the Missouri* in person, because our president (another populist) so badly managed our pandemic that no museum in North Carolina is open to the public this spring, but I keep an image of it on my laptop screen. I chose this painting because I am preoccupied by natural disasters and the climate crisis—not represented here, but evoked, at least for me. From an environmental point of view, Benton's painting reads as interestingly contemporary, or at least familiar. The Missouri River experienced eight months of flooding in 2019; aerial photos show street signs, rooftops, treetops peeking out of muddy floodwater. There are no people in these photos—the people have fled, or have been evacuated.

When I'm not looking at my computer image of *Spring on the Missouri*, a curious thing happens: in my mind I see a woman loading the cart in the foreground. She wears a blue dress and a hat, and her ankles are spattered with mud. She is curvy and solid. Maybe she is a composite: of Andrew Wyeth's or Edward Hopper's women, or a woman from one of Benton's other paintings, dancing to the "old music" he loved.

Maybe, in part, she is me, fleeing from Hurricane Florence with my husband and our two little daughters in 2018. We packed up our hatchback when the whole state was colored red on the threat map, and then drove west. In three days, Florence swamped North Carolina's coast with more than thirty inches of rain. I remember watching my daughters sleep in the dim light of a friend's guest room, and feeling both lucky and afraid.

Like Benton, who often painted rivers and saw them as a kind of escape, I am drawn to water that can carry you from one place to the next. I've almost always lived close enough to a river that I can walk to see it every day—Virginia's tidal Mattaponi, where I grew up; the East River in New York, which coursed by my Brooklyn neighborhood; the rocky and temperamental Haw River in North Carolina, where I live now. I've learned to monitor the Haw's condition as our storms have increased in frequency and severity. As we waited for Florence to pass, I lay sleeplessly holding my phone each night, refreshing weather reports and USGS gauges. How badly would the Haw flood? Would the Haw, so shallow my daughters wade in it in good weather, wash out its high bridges?

Almost, not quite. Next time.

Ben Berns
Swamp Mallows

1995
Oil on canvas
52 1/16 × 90 1/16 in.
Purchased in memory of William Luther Staton (1871–1944) and Mattie Worsley Staton (1882–1963) with funds from their daughter Mary Lois Staton

Gibbons Ruark

Swamp Mallows

Nearly still water winding among the grasses.
Low white clouds of blossoms, "useless for picking
Since they wilt within an hour." A cumulous sky.
This looks so much like a version of the calm
We might slip into out of troubled waters,

You will forgive me if I sense my father
Just out of sight around some mallowy bend.
At the painting's edges time unravels anyway,
So we might as well let it be summer,
Eastern Carolina, 1949,

The moment he leans down to steady the johnboat
Beside the dock for me to clamber into.
Then, when he has me balanced in the bow,
He reaches me the rods and tackle box
And steps down gingerly into the business end.

This time he has only a single paddle.
We won't be going far, and he loves the quiet
As the boat ripples into a channel
So narrow we can touch the brush on either side.
Then it is all drift and fish—the sun lowering,

The "weedless" hooked lines skimming the bottom for bream—
Casting and reeling till down the long perspective
Of the evening we grow weary of fishing
And catching nothing, lay the gear down carefully
In the slick boat-bottom and give in to drift.

My father's hat is tilted over his eyes
As we float in the freedom of saying nothing
Till warmth and water ferry us into a drowse.
Anybody watching from the bank would see us
Slide unknowingly under a little footbridge

Where a few old ones with kerchiefs on their heads
Are lifting their crab lines with the patience of heaven,
And then we scrape a tree stump and wake up to this:
Nearly still water winding among the grasses.
Low white clouds of blossoms. A cumulous sky.

We have come around in a backwater silence
Still white with mallows. In the face of all this air
And water and slow-to-perish brightness,
We might for once imagine death has been neglectful
And surrendered our passage to be banked with bloom.

Luis Egidio Meléndez
Still Life with Game

circa 1770
Oil on canvas
14⁹⁄₁₆ × 19³⁄₈ in.
Purchased with funds from the North Carolina State Art Society (Robert F. Phifer Bequest)

Jim Grimsley

Walk through Birdland

HOW THE DEAD can love you. Stop. How the dead can love you when you. Stop talking. Why they take you into the yard when they do. Stop. Listen. The neighbor is always listening, walking past the house without any real reason. We are among the living and the, all the living and the. Other ones. And. When they want to, when they rise up, how they can love you, forever.

You have had bad news. You will stop talking, shut your mouth. You will lie down in the field and your heart will gather up in one knot. Flatten your palm against your mouth and bite the skin enough to feel your teeth. Your heart will gather. Shut your mouth up in one knot. Never open anything else. Die down in the field. Hard as a bone you will be one knot.

But today we will walk through the world, into the shadowed space between the house and the abandoned yard. Lately we have been smelling the dead in the yard next door, the ones they found and the ones they didn't. The smell lingers, incredible pulsation, as if the rotting is a kind of life. As if the smell of decay has become an emanation of waves over the grass where the dead were found. Abandoned, in the yard next door, along the yard next door, you and I, we are walking ... Then

From above they are

Showering down they are

Showering down onto the yard they are falling out of the sky they are raining through the bare branches onto the leaves onto the ground where there they are, all the grackles in the world, all the glossy grackles with blueblack heads diving and showering down through the air in the late. Searching for pecans among the unraked leaves, the birds are chattering and chiding one another, talking about that last hop, whether they are headed in the right direction, shoving and digging their beaks into the leaf humus, searching. For food is everything this time of year. Their hearts are beating furiously and yet the flock seems relaxed. The grackles take everything in stride, lifting in waves as you pass, as I pass, the one of us. We are walking through the birds, through the midst of them, and they are accepting of us, and we are one, and everything is at peace within us. We are even inside the birds and they are inside us and everything is at peace. It is a walk through birdland and we stop.

In the yard. Where they are crawling over

My feet. The birds are crawling over my feet now. But farther ahead in the yard

Then down the street he is. He is always walking past the house without any real reason. When he walks to town he never brings anything back. And the birds are crawling over my feet and they are in the high grass ahead of me in the abandoned yard and of course you will not look, you refuse, you always leave the hard part of looking to me.

:Where the birds are crawling over the dead. Who can love you. Even so. With the grackles crawling over your face. The blueblackheaded birds, all of them, the world's whole population of them, crawling over your face, and you are dead, and they are not above eating you. Already, the eyes and face have suffered battery. It is no wonder you do not sit up, you dead one. It is no wonder you hide your face beneath the mask of feathers.

The neighbor passes and he sees you looking and you say, we say, we two as one, "Here's another dead one. Look."

"Yes, there's another one," the neighbor agrees.

"This one's good and dead."

"Yes, this one's good and dead."

"So," I say, and you are, naturally, hiding within; you are always quailing and hiding within at times like these;

"So," I say, "what am I supposed to do about it? I'm already late for work as it is." (A whole day late. As it is.) But anyway,

"I suppose you should call whoever you call. The ones who find dead bodies." The neighbor spoke mildly but in a clipped way.

"They already went through this yard this week," I said, slipping into the past tense myself, feeling the narrative gather force around me. "With a fine-tooth comb, they said. Those ones you were talking about, I forget the name." Sighing, firmly anchored in the past now, becoming "he." Becoming fully third person, like the neighbor. He and the neighbor stood in the yard looking at the dead one in the grass. The self-integrating sight of the dead and in fact stinking-dead corpse in the grass with the hundreds of millions of birds crawling over it and through it, very nearly through it, he and the neighbor watched this image.
The neighbor sighed and said, "It's always like this."

"What did he die of?"

The neighbor sighed again. "That thing everybody dies of. Probably."

The moment became perfect, the story culminating in the walk of the neighbor away from the yard, gloriously serene, in the golden slanting bar of a sunbeam lancing through the gap of dormers across the street, the golden lance slashing onto the neighbor, illuminating him in one final resplendent burst, a halo of alabaster fire. "It's always like this," the neighbor had said.

Even then slipping, though. I am slipping back. I am not sure if the neighbor is really gone or whether he was ever really there. I know I was never "he." I am looking at the dead one who is approaching the upright position slowly. Tedious, when the limbs no longer bend, to get up off the ground like this. But this is the gift of the dead to the living, occasionally to stand upright. We are taking the hand of the dead one, which is cold, we are walking with the grackles perched on our shoulders, heads and arms, this is the real ending, there is no narrative, we are only here, where the dead can love you sometimes, forever sometimes, in birdland.

Ed Ruscha
Scratches on the Film

1993
Acrylic on canvas
36 1/16 × 72 in.
Purchased with funds from the North Carolina Museum of Art Foundation, Art Trust Fund

Nickole Brown

Endling

1.

As in *ender*. As in *relict*. Or as in *terminarch*, a word that has the dank
smell of the queen and all her bees dead—as in ended, as in the last of,

a kind not just *functionally* over but *officially* so, that last
scratched frame reeling past, the whip of the reel whipping
round and round.

Oh, we know, we know—we've read
the credits—the story's over—
but still, we satisfy ourselves with the flash
of those final words: *the end.*

2.

As in Martha, a passenger once so star-numerous
it was a cinch to club them from the sky with the same skillet
used to fry them in, to club and club until there was
not one left to eat, just Martha, that dun-colored bird
done, the one named when we could have named the countless
that came before, that bird named too

late who fell dead from a low perch
at the Cincinnati Zoo. Afraid she'd spoil on the long ride, they held her
upside-down by her feet, encased her in the tight fist
of a three-hundred-pound block of ice, put her on a fast train
for the capital of the country that killed her kind because

they could, that ate flock after flock and fed the rest to
their hogs. A good hundred years later, I saw her or at least her
display, the amber beads used to replace her eyes
a dusty, muddied glass, a fake
taxidermist stare that stared back at nothing, reflected back
only the dumb reflection of me.

3.

Or as in another colonial name—
not Martha, as in the dead wife of, but George, as in the dead
man himself, our first first family aptly
laying claim. Yes, George, a tree snail once so abundant
its shells clattered strands of Hawaiian leis, or as in another
George, the last tortoise of another island that died

the same blister of a summer I took a deep south train far
north, a romantic cliché slapped down when the train ahead
was knocked over, its cart pushed off track and on its side
helpless as any flipped tortoise.

Thirteen hours we breathed each other's stench
before the crew let the suffocating lot of us stumble out
stunned by sun somewhere in a God-only-knows-where-
Indiana cornfield. I didn't know shit about tortoises then
and certainly not a thing about old George, nor did I know
then that men once lugged tortoises just like him to their ships,
stacking them shell-down, leaving them to kick their legs
helpless, storing them alive until it was time
to eat. No, I didn't know, I didn't,

and in the screaming cicada waves of that field, a man stood
beside me, told me his *place was drowned years back by that bitch
Katrina*, said *ain't right, ain't right*, before reaching
into the socket of his jaw to plier out a tooth with pointer and thumb.

I don't remember much else except the desperate
extraction's suck and pop, how he pitched the tooth
into farmland so dry that bad seed bounced and rolled
between rows of scorched corn as if the ground were polished
concrete. The man was the first refugee

of climate change I'd met, and it was then I knew
our trip wasn't just waylaid by one freak wind
but the same wind caught in sails to push
those men to what they called a
new world even though it had existed long before
them, that the storm that took that man's home was begun
long ago, was one of many vicious
sisters of that Monsanto field dying in drought.

4.
Yes, an end, an endling, the very end
tickled with an extra syllable, the end sweetened
with *ling*, making an ender sound elvish, pure
unicorn, more newborn than what it is—a baby's

opposite, not just an animal dead but dead-
dead, more un-done than unborn. As in Celia, another lonely
last of her kind, an Ibex, which sounds like a sports car but was
a mountain goat, a breed hunted to just this
one until that flashing light for her tracking device stood still
on the screen, confirming what we knew
would come. As in her great horn
snapped in half by a falling tree—how I can't understand
that image, how an impossible—that gut vulnerability hidden
within such tough bone, the horn snapped in half
revealing not a bone broken through like you'd think but a limp
muscle of pink flopped like a tongue car-struck. As in Celia,

not brought back exactly but resurrected or at least
needled into returning, a fetus
teased into living with the ice and electricity of bright white
coats. As in that clone, *her kid* if you can call her hers,
that wet baby who lived

minutes, her malformed lungs calling her back to the water
from which she'd just risen. As in Celia, Celia 2.0, if you want to make her
into a joke, Saint Not-Quite-Celia of Seven Minutes—a time too long
for a phone's video clip but too short to give that miracle—the end
of an endling—her own name.

5.

Listen. What I'm trying to say has something
to do with how our hunger has made us
sick, how wrong it is that we only give an individual animal
a name until the end, damn near the opposite of how we name

our own, all those ultrasound expectations
swaddled with a name before they've even crowned, all those names
in books peddled when I was a kid next to the t.v. guide and candy
cigarettes. Even those who wait to give a name until a baby's sure

to live—afraid to name a being that might not even
become—are closer to doing it right, because here we name animals
right before they go
extinct. I mean, yes, there is *bird*—a word even babies learn—
and yes, we look into the yard and name *cardinal*, say
dusty red, mute-colored and *thus female*, but who am I
this summer, watching that one who shimmies and jives
in the bird bath before lifting her clean, wet body up to a branch,
her blood-bright mate a good guardian, perched nearby and waiting
until she's dry before he takes his own bath? I mean, who am I to call her

a bird or a cardinal, to say *morning, little birdie*, without learning
who she is, this one bird, right there, not just on a branch, but on *the*
bare branch of a dying willow in my yard?

As in you, little one, tell me: what is your name?
There are others of your kind here, but I won't let it fool me
into believing they're the same, won't let myself dismiss you
again with a quick *red bird* as if there's an infinite of you,
because there's only one, and there you are. Because if we don't
change, if I don't change, your death, which is sure to come
just as my own, could be not just an end but the end,
the picture finally over and all of us exiting this theater
with our faces in our hands.

Ursula von Rydingsvard
Ogromna

2009
Cedar and graphite
H. 20 ft. 7 in × W. 12 ft. 4 in. × D. 11 ft. 8 in.
Commissioned with funds from the North Carolina
State Art Society (Robert F. Phifer Bequest)

Tyree Daye

Instructions

An upside-down mountain top,
ancestors as tornado,
a wooden drill
to run your hands over
in the dark. A place for us
to gather, together.
Build something bigger than the I
God told my hands
to labor.

Chris Drury
Cloud Chamber for the Trees and Sky

2003
Stone, wood, and turf
Approx. diam. 12 ft.
Commissioned by the North Carolina Museum of Art with funds from
the North Carolina State Art Society (Robert F. Phifer Bequest)

Helena Feder

Cloud Chamber

for A. R. Ammons (on Chris Drury's camera obscura)

Down in the summer canopy
a stone grown so green you'd
miss it but for the door ajar

until you are inside: push hard
and something ancient floods
that was always waiting there:

a deep emptiness in the dark
solid ground a mountain cold
as in the beginning: then a nearing,

an almost, light's softest shadow
warm as we imagine cave paintings
by the fires that lit their way:

the leaf gardens on the walls
flicker, float, and fade.
Here even the air breathes.

Reach, root this thirst from
bare bracken feet to the heart
rushing in your ears,

offer to the chambered sky all
your growing things like flowers
thrown to a performance:

in this wood quiet dim
sanctuary is the light
that lifts our skin.

Philipp Stenglin
Torah Pointer

1717–21
Silver: hollow-formed, cast, chased
L. 15 3/16 in.
Gift of the Friends of the Judaic Art Gallery in memory of Barry S. Fine

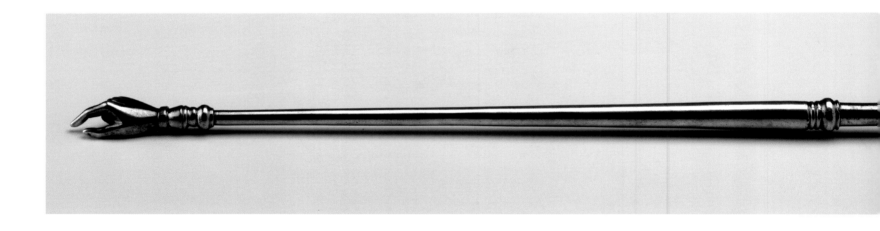

Jessica Jacobs

Make a fence

around the Torah, said the rabbis. *Something there is
that doesn't love a wall,* said Frost. Yet this world
is lousy with them. More than we can count

on our dog walk alone, chainlink and trellis and white
wooden pickets. Fences to keep people's bad barking dogs
in, to keep our bad barking dog out. His nostrils flaring

wide as a twirled skirt as he reads the tales of past passersby
on the fences that mark what is another's burden, another's
privilege to tend, and what is open to the traffic of strangers.

Called before the Torah, a reader tracks the cramped letters
with a yad, a metal pointer topped by a tiny pointing hand.
If it feels colder than the air, it's because silver steals

your body's heat, this tool to keep your place, keep you
in your place, to keep you from marring even a single sacred letter.
This, one fence among many: Do not bring the Torah

in the bathroom, do not sit beside it on a bench, do not stand before it
naked (lest you be buried naked, stripped of all the good you did).
But sometimes barriers grow so large it's hard to see

what they're protecting. And here is the fig tree yearning
past its fence, reaching toward the walk with its fat-fingered leaves.
Here, the arbor propping branches slumped as the shoulders

of a weary giant—yet under its hunch, an exuberance of mulberries.
There, the yellow house whose bramble is more than worth its thorns:
drops of wet ink drip from the branches, blackberries beckoning us

to make a quill of our tongues. Every fence in my mind has a gate.
One with an easy latch and well-oiled hinges. And our neighbors
urge us to indulge—*There's more than we can possibly eat*—so

here, love, is fruit with the sun still inside it. Let me
thumb the juice from your chin. Let us honor what we love
                                        by taking it in.

Francesco Francia
Madonna and Child with Two Angels

circa 1495–1500
Oil on panel
34¾ × 22¼ in.
Gift of The Samuel H. Kress Foundation

Joseph Bathanti

Madonna and Child with Two Angels

THAT'S CLAIRE RAFFO, as the Blessed Mother, in the eighth-grade play.

Of all the girls, she radiated that wistful Italian Renaissance gaze, the aching Madonna piety: chaste mouth, hooded almond eyes, flawless complexion, a luminous, stained-glass iconography that murmured tragically from within.

But there's also that unmistakable, embarrassed smirk, the boredom those Italian girls from East Liberty, when forced to pose, affect. Claire isn't one of the really hard ones. She doesn't brawl or carry a switchblade. She's been assigned *Pride and Prejudice*, but she's hidden *The Bell Jar* and *Ariel* in her purse. She smokes Kools and has fallen, regrettably, for Allen Compton, a cur, a real *gavone*—in truth an apprentice assassin, all black leather, the aftermath of *West Side Story*, without the music, without the poetry. She'll realize these things later about him, but by then it will be too late.

Claire as Mary—almost a joke, a satire only she is aware of—but she admires how she looks in the costume: velvet and silk brocade robes and *gonnelle*—cobalt, incarnadine, emerald. The white *camicia* that peeks from her left sleeve. The lace headdress beneath the veil. Melodramatic cascades of fabric. The golden nimbus affixed to her head—cardboard, yes, but it seems to float above her of its own volition. There is decided cachet in being the Mother of God, chosen above all others. Angelically, Sister Hyancinth, who is no angel, plays the harp and sings *Regina Coeli* in her unearthly soprano, so ethereal the crows in the May sycamores just beyond the sash turn to ash and a sudden wind whips up.

Claire knows what's coming. She's read all about it in the Gospels. One unthinkable Friday, thirty-three years down the road, she'll be forced to keep vigil at the foot of the cross as chubby, blond Yeshua, the Jewish infant on her lap, falsely accused, then tortured—a put-up job by the State—is executed by crucifixion.

Despite the hard times ahead, Claire loves having the naked Prince of Peace in her lap, the flame-orange rosary she looped around his neck. Where the baby came from remains a mystery, but it's clear He's a born iconoclast, androgynous, already composing *The Beatitudes*. That raised right hand: Is it Benediction? Reckoning? It won't be long before He's lean, hard as a hammer—*like a thief in the night*—His open palm clenched in the righteous fist of revolution.

The blue-winged angels are Nicolina Russo and Davida Pofi, Claire's bodyguards, and best friends—two girls not to mess with—also chosen for their looks. They're whispering. After the play, they've schemed to meet Junior Rancatore and Joe Brush in Junior's pink Chevy II and catch *Easy Rider* at Silver Lake Drive-In, under the Larimer Bridge, on Washington Boulevard. They don't get to have haloes.

Beyond Nicolina and Davida looms the unimaginable: shimmering lawns, luscious trees, like the vast yards Claire's father, a landscaper—an *animale* Claire despises—frets over and makes so beautiful for the rich in Highland Park and Fox Chapel. At the edge of the ether resides the legendary biblical firmament and atop it the *della robbia* sky. The vaults of Heaven are up there, and some pretty little clouds, cumulonimbi, not bothering a soul, into which Claire, the Madonna, exempt from death, will one day be assumed.

Jan Steen
The Worship of the Golden Calf

circa 1672–75
Oil on canvas
70¼ × 61¼ in.
Purchased with funds from
the State of North Carolina

Ben Johnston-Krase

On Jan Steen's *The Worship of the Golden Calf*

For the record, it was never really about the calf.
Had we known this would be part of the Ten Commandments story
we might have opted
for something more becoming of "Thou shalt not commit adultery."
But there we were
and who were we to know?

You can only live on manna for so long
or so we thought:
turned out there was plenty to eat
whole vats of soup,
fruit to cook, fruit to cut,
fruit to crush sticky and drop where we stood.

Might we agree that once in a while
the holiest thing we can do
is gather our every scrap of gold
into one community pot
to be melted and shaped and loved
into something frivolous?

So that we can say
together and with lusty confidence:
We have breath.
Our lives are our own.

The curve of this naked pale shoulder:
is it not the sacrament of this wilderness moment?

Govert Flinck
The Return of the Prodigal Son

circa 1640–42
Oil on canvas
52¹¹/₁₆ × 67⅜ in.
Purchased with funds from the State of North Carolina

156

Joseph Millar

Govert Flinck's *The Return of the Prodigal Son*

In this one the father
has not ridden out
into the fields to meet him.
He steps down from the porch
opening his arms
to the one kneeling there,
barefoot in his ragged shirt
being barked at by the dog

and the older brother
at the window above,
his face a pale
and dissatisfied blotch,
the brow pinched in, angry
at the way love
transcends the bonds of duty,
no matter how long the two shepherds below
have tended their tiny flock
and how long the water has fallen
from the dark cask the man
in the shadows
keeps pouring into the trough.

Gilliam Hornstein
The Light and the Dying

20th century
Oil on canvas
48 × 32 in.
Gift of Carl M. Kirby, Jr., and
Mr. and Mrs. Thomas Kirby

Lawrence Naumoff

The Light and the Dying

THE HAY WAS CUT. It was dry. It lay loose and thin and here and there had streaks of pale green, though mostly it was tan and tasseled on the ends. His neighbor didn't own a baler, so it needed pitching into a wagon. He had traded labor with his neighbor, who would paint the room, and then he would help with the hay.

The weather was cool. It was a good day to work.

His neighbor had persuaded him to paint the room blue. Not an angry blue, and not a heavy navy blue, but a blue that was like the beginning of the day, the neighbor had said, and then the man had waited for the word, ethereal, but it didn't come. Rather, his neighbor said, a blue as if it had been there for 50 years—, the blue of his wife's eyes?—he wondered, but it didn't turn out to be that color, either. It was simply a very washed and very light blue, as if the paint were slowly dying, but with dignity, as if, actually, and simply, it had been on his wall for 50 years.

Now, as he sat in the corner waiting to be called to help, it was almost as if he had become the color himself, his shirt, the tablecloth, the floor, the background of the portrait, all of it as restful as a baby under a blue blanket.

He could see, across the room, through the window, his neighbor getting ready. Over the years, he had noticed that the neighbor had to paint almost everything, so that once he painted it, he could then live it, having already been there. Was that it?

They had already walked through the loose hay. It was perfect to get up today, to get up now, not tomorrow, but today. Maybe the room, which was that tender blue, made the hay special, silk soft and smelling like lavender.

He went outside. He got the pitchfork. He stood in front of his house. He waited.

The weather was cool. The hay was dry. The room was blue. It was a good day to work.

Winslow Homer
Weaning the Calf

1875
Oil on canvas
24 × 38 in.
Purchased with funds from the State of North Carolina

James Applewhite

On Winslow Homer's *Weaning the Calf*

What shadows my happiness? The boy and calf so linked by
      a rope seem to forget all else. Grass recedes to the horizon
and chickens roam free. Hay stacked richly as memory bulges
          mountainously on the sky.

My wish is matched by this scene, where green reflected in
      aqua and clouds lets the perspective between take sight into
a vapor refusing to be mist, a balmy air which will not weep
          but reveal: two town boys in hats

and suspenders, bystanders, who also look past the other boy concealed
      in a ragged shade. His brother the calf resists being hauled
from its source. Here the grass with its highlights, sunflakes like
          the whites of chickens and cow and

of splashes on a boy and the calf's legs, seems mother of everything—
      this vista between the framing trees, where farms and towns
hover as invisibly as sorrow is in this air, as if seasons were
          only apparent. Yet the cow being

led away switches her tail, tossing her head back lyrically so
     that the arc of her horns pinpoints the clouds. What forgetfulness
of vines twists this open fence not enclosing one earth-breast,
        where red on a rooster's combs and on

the farther chickens leads my eye into a landscape without limit?
     I trust in it, give myself to the summer as if breathing it,
this American horizon. Yet the farmhand leaning hard to pull the cow
        away remains as faceless as seasons.

His figure cannot go home, for Homer has not painted those houses
     hidden by borders. The gesture of this white mother's neck
sharpens her horns so that they pierce me with loss. The dark boy cannot
        follow, as spring does winter,

beyond concern, assumed, too close to see. Part of the farm.
     Now I grasp his braced legs, work-strengthened shoulders,
the curve of his back and neck, though his face is averted.
        The rest is pastoral, a tale of expanse

and ease not purchased by any expense of breath. I turn away,
     the points of hurt in my chest an ache after beauty: almost grasped,
like ice, composed to last. I feel it melt into a world where
        sun conceals its shade, and seasons pass.

Richard Wilson

An Extensive Landscape with Cottages near a Lake

circa 1744–45
Oil on canvas
32 × 49⅛ in.
Purchased with funds from the State of North Carolina, by exchange, and the North Carolina State Art Society (Robert F. Phifer Bequest), in memory of Richard S. Schneiderman, Director of the North Carolina Museum of Art

Ross White

IN DISPRAISE OF PASTORAL

The sheep have grazed until the grass
sighs with numb uniformity.

The sheepdog pads around the lake,
his charges too content to wander.

The boughs bloom with leaves
like wax in predictable patterns.

In every paradise,
someone dies of boredom.

The coral bells sigh out dull pink.
The lake cannot be troubled to ripple.

Is it any wonder the woman
washing clothes dreams of volcanoes?

Is it any wonder that when the child
sees the prospector, she envies the rifle?

Bwa peoples, Burkina Faso
Bush Buffalo Mask

20th century
Wood, paint, and string
H. 17¾ × W. 8¾ × D. 7¾ in.
Gift of the Hanes Corporation

Jessica Q. Stark

The Wild Water Buffalo

are both diurnal and nocturnal,
which may seem contradictory
aside from my mother whistling

into another life around the
kitchen island, the night sky
barely breaking into dawn.

Sleep is a luxury for the unmasked,
small territory of the ever-on-
time, monolingual, monopoly

tenderfoots of the land & soot.
Once in a sojourn from
responsibility I traveled

to my mother's country, drank
the water and fell ill for four days.
In the eternal break of my fever,

we hiked to a riverbed for a bath—
the sweet, cool slip on my skin.

I submerged into another view,

I broke water and met eyes with
a frightening mass, half-submerged
under our murky blanket.

Bathing with a beast is no burden.

And how many ways can
you break a mask? How many

syllables would it take to
break from one's own stubborn
and beastly tongue?

Roman
Portrait of the Emperor
Marcus Aurelius

Late 2nd century
Marble
H. 27¾ × W. 18½ × D. 12½ in.
Purchased with funds from gifts by
Mr. and Mrs. Gordon Hanes,
Mrs. Chauncey McCormick, and
various donors, by exchange